THE 2009
Solo and Small Firm
Legal Technology Guide

CRITICAL DECISIONS MADE SIMPLE

By Sharon D. Nelson, Esq., John W. Simek, and Michael C. Maschke

Introduction by Ross L. Kodner, Esq.

LAW PRACTICE MANAGEMENT SECTION

MARKETING • MANAGEMENT • TECHNOLOGY • FINANCE

Commitment to Quality: The Law Practice Management Section is committed to quality in our publications. Our authors are experienced practitioners in their fields. Prior to publication, the contents of all our books are rigorously reviewed by experts to ensure the highest quality product and presentation. Because we are committed to serving our readers' needs, we welcome your feedback on how we can improve future editions of this book.

Cover design by Jim Colao.

Library of Congress Cataloging-in-Publication Data
The 2009 Solo and Small Firm Legal Technology Guide: Critical Decisions Made Simple. Sharon Nelson, John Simek and Michael Maschke: Library of Congress Cataloging-in-Publication Data is on file.

ISBN: 978-1-60442-321-1

Discounts are available for books ordered in bulk. Special consideration is given to state bars, CLE programs, and other bar-related organizations. Inquire at Book Publishing, American Bar Association, 321 N. Clark Street, Chicago, Illinois 60654.

Dedication

SHARON D. NELSON AND John W. Simek dedicate this book to all of their professional colleagues who have shared so generously their compendium of legal tech knowledge for years. Thanks to Jim Calloway, Tom Mighell, Dennis Kennedy, Craig Ball, Ross Kodner, Laura Calloway, Reid Trautz, Dave Ries, Tina Ayiotis, Bruce Dorner, Bruce Olson, Dan Pinnington, Dave Bilinsky, Ben Schorr, Joe Kashi, Andy Adkins, Tom O'Connor, David Masters, and the list goes on. Without the camaraderie of our own personal "Geek Squad," it would be impossible to even try to keep up with the legal tech blitzkrieg.

Michael C. Maschke dedicates this book to his wife, family, and friends, and to the support that they have provided over the past year, allowing the process of writing a book to be an enjoyable escape from the realities of everyday life. He would also like to dedicate this book to the rest of the staff members at Sensei, who like having a good time and enjoy mind-numbing conversations about anything technology related.

Contents at a Glance

Contents

About the Authors

Sharon D. Nelson, Esq.

 Sharon D. Nelson is the President of Sensei Enterprises, Inc. Ms. Nelson graduated from Georgetown University Law Center in 1978 and has been in private practice ever since. She now focuses exclusively on electronic evidence law.

Ms. Nelson and Mr. Simek are the co-editors of the law and technology newsletter *Bytes in Brief*. Ms. Nelson, Mr. Simek and Mr. Maschke are the co-authors of the 2008 edition of this book. They also wrote *Information Security for Lawyers and Law Firms* (American Bar Association, 2006). Additionally, Ms. Nelson and Mr. Simek coauthored *The Electronic Evidence and Discovery Handbook: Forms, Checklists, and Guidelines* (American Bar Association, 2006). Their articles have appeared in numerous national publications.

Ms. Nelson is the past President of the Fairfax Bar Association, a Director of the Fairfax Law Foundation, and past chair of the American Bar Association's TECHSHOW® Board. She currently serves on the Governing Council of the ABA's Law Practice Management Section and as chair of its Publications Board. She is a member of ARMA's E-Discovery Advisory Board, a member of the ABA's Advisory Panel, and a member of the Editorial Board of the ABA's *The Practical Litigator* magazine. She is a graduate of Leadership Fairfax. She serves on the governing Council of the Virginia State Bar, its Mandatory Continuing Legal Education Board, and its Unauthorized Practice of Law Committee. She is the chair of the Virginia State Bar's Committee on Technology in Law Practice. She is a member of the

American Bar Association, the Virginia Bar, the Virginia Bar Association, and the Fairfax Bar Association.

John W. Simek

 Mr. Simek is the Vice President of Sensei Enterprises, Inc. He is an EnCase Certified forensic technologist (EnCE). Mr. Simek has a national reputation as a computer forensics technologist and has testified as an expert witness throughout the United States.

Mr. Simek holds a degree in engineering from the United States Merchant Marine Academy and an MBA in finance from Saint Joseph's University. After forming Sensei, he ended his 20+ year affiliation with Mobil Oil Corporation, where he served as a senior technologist designing and troubleshooting Mobil's networks throughout the western hemisphere. Mr. Simek has in-depth experience with network troubleshooting, hardware and software implementations, systems integration, and logistical and financial expertise in a wide range of computer engineering designs and solutions. He has an extensive knowledge of multiprotocol environments and a diverse range of networking technologies. In addition to his EnCase Certification (EnCE), Mr. Simek is a Certified Handheld Examiner, Certified Novell Engineer, Microsoft Certified Professional + Internet, Microsoft Certified Systems Engineer, NT Certified Independent Professional, and a Certified Internetwork Professional. He is also a member of the High Tech Crime Network and of the International Information Systems Forensics Association as well as the American Bar Association. He is a member of the ABA Law Practice Management Publications Board and an Advisory Board member for the ABA's Law Practice TODAY webzine. He currently provides information technology support to over 220 area law firms, legal entities and corporations. He is a co-author of The Electronic Evidence and Discovery Handbook: Forms, Checklists and Guidelines (American Bar Association, 2006), Information Security for Lawyers and Law Firms (American Bar Association, 2006), The 2008 Solo and Small Firm Legal Technology Guide: Critical Decisions Made Simple (American Bar Association, 2008) and a contributing author of eDiscovery (Pennsylvania Bar Institute, 2008). He is a frequent author and speaker on legal technology and electronic evidence throughout the country.

Mr. Simek's contact information:

John W. Simek
Vice President, Sensei Enterprises, Inc.
3975 University Dr., Suite 225
Fairfax, VA. 22030
703-359-0700 (phone)
703-359-8434 (fax)
jsimek@senseient.com

Michael C. Maschke

Michael C. Maschke is the Director of Computer Forensics at Sensei Enterprises, Inc. He is an EnCase Certified forensic technologist (EnCE) and a Certified Computer Examiner (#744).

Mr. Maschke holds a degree in telecommunications from James Madison University, with a minor in computer science. Mr. Maschke has significant experience with network troubleshooting, design and implementation, systems integration, and computer engineering. He previously was the director of Sensei's information technology department, which provides support to more than 220 area law firms, legal entities, and corporations.

Mr. Maschke is a Microsoft Certified Systems Engineer (2000/2003), Microsoft Certified Professional, and a Microsoft Certified Systems Administrator. He has spoken at the American Bar Association's TECHSHOW® conference on information security and is a coauthor of *Information Security for Lawyers and Law Firms* (American Bar Association, 2006) and *The 2008 Solo and Small Firm Legal Technology Guide: Critical Decisions Made Simple* (American Bar Association, 2008).

Acknowledgments

FIRST, WE ARE VERY excited this year to have one the nation's finest legal technology consultants, Ross L. Kodner, Esq., as the author of the introduction to this book and the author of the Paper LESS chapter. He is the president of MicroLaw, a noted Wisconsin legal technology firm founded in 1985, with clients nationwide. Mr. Kodner's contribution to legal technology knowledge can't be overstated—his compendium of writings, his lectures, and his willingness to help one and all through the ABA's Solosez listserv have all contributed to a stellar reputation. His knowledge runs broad and deep, and we are so delighted that he also offered to contribute a chapter on the Paper Less® Office. Mr. Kodner originated this concept and has been a missionary on its behalf for as many years as we can remember. It was some years back that he was kind enough to recommend authors Sharon D. Nelson and John W. Simek as potential ABA TECHSHOW speakers. They gratefully acknowledge their debt to him—it is fitting that the three of us are still, after all this time, good friends and colleagues, who continue to collaborate in the ever-evolving world of legal tech.

Thanks, Ross, for being such an invaluable part of this edition.

As always, we must thank Tim Johnson, the executive editor of LPM Publishing for encouraging our concept of an annual publication devoted to the fast-moving world of legal technology, and specifically targeting solos and small firms. For years, this concept languished, but thanks to Tim, it was resurrected. We are working hard to keep it current. Tim, your hard work and professionalism have made the entire project a joy from beginning to end—thank you, thank you, thank you!

Thanks to our fantastic book production manager, Denise Constantine, and our editorial assistant, Kimia Shelby. As always, the LPM Publishing staff is a joy to work with.

We are very grateful to our good friend, Dave Ries, an extraordinary litigator in Pittsburgh and a terrific self-taught technologist, who served as project manager for this book. His suggestions and thoughts enriched the final product immeasurably.

Thanks to Sensei's marketing director, Charles Wagner, for proofing our copy and keeping us straight.

Finally, we thank our colleagues here at Sensei, who carried the load while we were writing and were never too busy to deliberate over recommendations and offer insightful comments. We don't come to work every day; we come to play, and we really like the folks we play with. Thanks, one and all!

Michael C. Maschke
Sharon D. Nelson
John W. Simek

Preface to the Second Edition

THANKS TO ALL THE readers who wrote us last year expressing their appreciation for our book. As we told you last year, we knew that any first effort to put together a succinct guide to legal technology for solos and small firms would have its rough edges. We are grateful for all the kind words and encouragement we received. We are even more grateful for those of our readers who took the time to make suggestions for improving this edition—we listened and incorporated many of them.

Just as a reminder, the premise of this book is simple. We want to help solo and small firm lawyers find the "sweet spot" of legal tech—the best value for the dollars. You don't need a Porsche, and the Hyundais don't have a great reputation for reliability, but there is a happy medium—professional-grade hardware and software that doesn't cost an arm and a leg.

As an annual guide, this book will never be more than several months behind the curve. If you can't afford your own legal technology consultant and are concerned about those who are selling snake oil, at least this book should provide you with a kind of "Consumer Reports" view of legal technology products.

We have no dog in the hunt—we have no financial or other interest in the advice we give. We could be wrong—dead wrong—but we are dead honest as well.

In this book we provide you with information and recommendations on computers, servers, networking equipment, legal software, cool gadgets for lawyers, and more. We take an in-depth look at the technologies that will be around in 2009 and provide information on how these technologies will shape the way solo and small firm decision makers think about their technology decisions in 2009.

Our recommendations are what we would do in a solo or small practice ourselves. Don't buy eMachines, and don't buy "Joe Chen" or other off-brand computers—do invest in quality technology that will have a good shelf life and serve you well so long as they live. And don't expect more than they can give. A server can be expected to last 4–5 years and a workstation or laptop 3–4. That's it folks. As the software also evolves, it demands ever more resources and the hardware ages both physically and in its ability to handle the new software. Remember the "Rule of Three" in upgrading—you should be upgrading one-third of your technology each year—sometimes you can stretch it to four—but if you try to limp along patching things with spit and promises, you are likely going to be in for a "big bang" upgrade, which is acutely painful for the average solo or small law firm. Leasing may help lessen this financial burden (at least on an annual basis), but you lose the option to change course quickly without the payment of penalty fees.

Be mindful of the fact that this book is written exclusively for solos and small law firms. There is no attempt to include big firm products or solutions. In addition, we have included our recommendations only, not "all available" products. If you don't see a product here, it is because that product is not among our usual recommendations. This is a "best of breed" selection to keep you from being confused by the veritable cornucopia of choices that exist.

We can't serve as your legal technology consultant unless you are in the Washington, D.C., area, but we are serious about our commitment to the legal profession and proud of our professional "giveback" through the ABA. If you have a question, we'll do our best to help. Just e-mail us at **sensei@senseient.com**. We appreciate all your comments and suggestions so that each subsequent edition can be better than the one before. Thanks, in advance, for your help!

Introduction

by Ross L. Kodner, Esq.

What a long, strange trip it's been.

"Truckin'"
The Grateful Dead

Jerry Garcia could very well have been describing the odyssey that is the legal technology marketplace and how it has developed over the last 30 years. In 1978, the most pioneering law practices were experimenting with the immediate ancestors of personal computers—systems from a variety of vendors that ran versions of CP/M, the "operating system that could have been." A year earlier, in 1977, two long-haired Silicon Valley wunderkinds named Steve Jobs and Steve Wozniak built the Apple II, which was effectively the first personal computer that emerged out of the digital primordial ooze of the CP/M days. Fast-forward four years and the personal computer went corporate—with IBM's ground-breaking IBM PC. The battle was joined, with the struggle being for the very hearts and minds of business users, including, of course, lawyers.

Think of all that has happened to legal technology and law practice computing since 1981 and those early days of the green-screen, 5-1/4″ dual floppy drive-equipped IBM PC. A few years later, we all were amazed by the document-drafting power of the elegant WordPerfect for DOS, renowned both for its clean, uncluttered electronic workspace and its "look under the hood and fix it" Reveal Codes function. In some ways, the famous WordPerfect clean-screen look foreshadowed an equally clean-screen giant, Google, and its elegantly spartan interface.

Consider the march of technology and how lawyers and law firms have adopted, acquired, upgraded to—and upgraded from—some of its key developments over the last 20 years:

- ♦ During the 1980s, CompuServe was the first electronic mail system and online resource for most of us.

I still remember my own CompuServe Information Service (CIS) ID: I was 94036,3223, communicating online at all of 300 baud in 1980. I was selling Radio Shack TRS-80 systems while an undergraduate student— the famous Model II was the high-end big seller in 1980. Little did we know that the IBM PC would burst on the scene the next year and kill the pioneering TRS-80 platform.

♦ Compaq introduced the first "IBM-compatible" portable computer in 1982. It weighed in at 35+ pounds and cost a shade over $4,000. We all coveted it.

I bought my first computer, a "portable" CP/M-based Kaypro II, in 1983, the summer before law school began. It was 34 lbs., equipped with 64K, dual 5-1/4" floppy drives to run my apps and save my documents, Word-Star as my word processor, and a hulking, grinding, table-shaking C.Itoh 60 lb. daisywheel printer. I was ready to take on law school in the age of personal computers.

♦ The first Macs appeared in 1984 and said "Hello."

♦ We watched the rise and fall of dedicated word processors such as CPT, with their marvelous, ground-breaking portrait-mode video displays, and of course, Wang systems.

I purchased my second computer, my first "IBM-compatible." As a poor law student, I was far from able to afford an actual IBM XT, the machine I lusted after with its 10-megabyte hard drive and a magnificent 5 lb. keyboard with keys that clicked, a Leading Edge Model D, replete with the latest in amber screen technology, a 20 MB hard drive, running MS-DOS. In 1985, my WordPerfect machine helped me complete law school and start my own legal technology business.

♦ Novell networking appeared in 1985.

I started my own firm, MicroLaw, the same year.

♦ Microsoft released Windows 1.0 in 1985. It didn't work. No one paid attention. Why would they when DOS worked so well— wasn't it all we needed? View the entire history of Windows at **http://www.microsoft.com/windows/WinHistoryDesktop.mspx**.

♦ CP/M, once the likely operating system for the future, died a quiet death in 1985.

♦ WordPerfect 4.2 appeared in 1986, revolutionizing word processing for law practices and businesses worldwide.

♦ In 1986, the first ABA TECHSHOW® was held in Chicago, giving the legal-technology marketplace a rallying point for information dissemination and education.

♦ In 1988, the precursor to today's dominant small firm legal document manager, Worldox, appeared in its DOS first versions as
Extend-a-File, working with WordPerfect 5.1 and Word for DOS.
Worldox helped bring file organization and "extended filenames"
to the frustrating and cryptic world of 8.3-character-format DOS
filenames.

♦ In 1989, DOS systems were honed to a near art form. With WordPerfect 5.2, the early Tabs 3 and Juris billing systems, WordPerfect Office
provided task-switching, calendars, and the famous mini-databases
called WordPerfect Notebooks, all balancing the bizarre PC memory
situations called Extended and Expanded memory. These were all
ways to use more than DOS's maximum addressable 640K of memory (which Bill Gates had proclaimed as being enough memory for
any computer, ever. Not!). It seemed things couldn't get much better.

♦ In the late 1980s, Abacus was the dominant case management system—the first commercially successful case information tracking
system in the DOS era.

♦ Windows 3.0 appeared in 1990, and everything changed. The world
of mainstream, mouse-driven graphical interfaces for business users
began. (Oddly, the Mac, so prevalent in "creative" environments,
had itself "leveraged" the GUI- and mouse-driven interface technology from Xerox's Palo Alto Research Center, or PARC. It had yet
to gain a foothold in the business marketplace and with its closed,
proprietary architecture, got sidestepped). Of course, the fact that
Windows 3.0 barely functioned and the cobbled-together hardware
support that nearly killed it made most of us in the fledging legal
technology industry afraid and confused.

♦ WordPerfect 5.2 appeared in 1992, and the first legal case management systems appeared—with STI's CaseMaster being one of the
very first. It ran on DOS, of course.

♦ In 1993, the first truly usable version of Windows appeared—version 3.1. The race was on in the modern era of graphical computing. Software vendors began a headlong rush to release Windows
versions of their software. Microsoft Office shipped "free" on new
computers, flooding the marketplace. WordPerfect got caught with
its pants down, and its version 5.2 for Windows functionally paled
in comparison to Microsoft Word 2.0 for Windows. Everyone
sensed that the beloved WordPerfect was in for trouble

♦ In 1995, the first 32-bit Windows system, called Windows 95,
appeared with the first iteration of such technologies as Plug and

Play (which most referred to as Plug and Pray), making it theoretically easier to attach and recognize peripherals such as scanners and printers. Microsoft Office 95 was the newly dominant office suite, largely on the basis of gaining market share through "free" bundling with new PC hardware. WordPerfect released its version 7 Suite, its first 32-bit edition, but had already lost market share to Microsoft Office. (It's hard to compete with "free.")

♦ In 1995 and 1996, the Internet, as we know it today, appeared. The first law firms registered domain names and the first law practice Web sites appeared. Lawyers jumped online with 2400-baud modems and via something called Trumpet Winsock managed to get online and start sending and receiving their first e-mails. The Internet era was upon us.

♦ *The Lawyer's Guide to the Internet*, by G. Burgess Allison, was published by the ABA Law Practice Management Section in March 1995.

My Paper LESS Office concept, subject of a chapter in this book, was unveiled in an article in Law Office Computing *magazine, providing law practices worldwide with a commonsense approach to using scanning technology to build complete electronic case files.*

♦ In 1996, the ABA established the Solosez listserv, later to become the ABA's largest online legal community, moving past the 3500-subscriber point in 2008.

♦ In 1996, the Technolawyer community gained an online foothold, continuing today as a powerhouse online legal technology resource under the tutelage of legal tech pioneer Neil Squillante and parent company Peerviews.

In 1997, my column, called "The Circuit Court," co-authored with Dan Coolidge and Bruce Dorner appeared in Law Office Computing *magazine, offering an irreverent view of legal technology—perhaps the first time the subject didn't take itself too seriously.*

♦ Also in 1997, Microsoft Office 97 ushered in the era of modern, do-everything, be-everything Office suites and, on the back of broad-bundled distribution, became the market leader for word processing. WordPerfect lost its market dominance and industry-standard status. New WordPerfect owner, Corel Corporation, valiantly believed it could compete head-to-head with Microsoft in spite of the latter's obvious advantage as the operating system developer.

♦ In 1997, this book's co-authors John Simek and Sharon Nelson formed Sensei Enterprises, a legal technology and computer forensics company, in Fairfax, Virginia.

◆ In October 1997, Andrew Z. Adkins, a legal technology consultant and the author of the ABA's *The Lawyer's Guide to Computerized Case Management Systems*, helped establish the Legal Technology Institute at the University of Florida Levin College of Law.

◆ Legal Windows applications became the norm with early Windows editions of case management systems appearing throughout the 1990s. The failure to release Windows versions of software was seen as an indication of technology incompetence. The still DOS-based Abacus practice management system, once dominant in the late 1980s and early 1990s, slipped behind to new upstarts such as Time Matters and Amicus Attorney.

◆ In 1999, legal case management was placed front and center with the bundling of Amicus Attorney with the Corel WordPerfect 8 Legal Suite.

◆ At the 2000 ABA TECHSHOW®, presenters Peter Krakauer and legal Internet marketing guru Greg Siskind announced that 10,000 law firms had Web sites.

◆ In 2000, the first attempts at Web-based legal software, called ASPs (Application Service Providers), were made, with West's WestWorks online case management system leading the charge. A year later, the ASP bubble spectacularly burst, with expensive product failures, largely due to the failure of the fledgling industry to address legal ethics and security issues. But it made a comeback in 2007, repackaged as SaaS (Software as a Service), with the first "successful" online practice management and billing systems. These included CaseManager Pro, Rocket Matter and Bill4Time.

◆ From 2000 to the present, a new era has ushered in modern case management systems with integrated systems from companies, including ProLaw and STI. The educational marketplace for technology CLE exploded; *Law Office Computing* magazine is at its height in disseminating information to small law practices, while *Law Technology News* speaks to mid-size and larger firms (while competing with each other for advertising dollars). Microsoft Office dominates the software marketplace for word processing, while WordPerfect valiantly soldiers on, still popular in small law practices.

◆ In 2000, metadata reared its head and electronic discovery burst into the public consciousness, as illustrated by a front page article in the October 20 issue of *The Wall Street Journal*, in which Donna Payne of the Payne Consulting Group was featured in an article on metadata. The litigation world would never be the same.

- In 2006, the era of legal social network and electronic collaboration took hold with lawyers using online services such as Facebook, LinkedIn, MySpace and Twitter.
- In 2008, the first edition of this book was published by the ABA Law Practice Management Section, bringing the subject of Legal Technology in a compendium/primer format to solo and small firm lawyers worldwide.
- For 2009 and beyond, the sky's the limit. Expect SaaS main-streamed, digital collaboration to become the norm rather than the exception, and legal blogging to hit Main Street lawyers as Yellow Page advertising dies away. Microsoft's SharePoint platform also will trickle down from the AMLAW 250 to Main Street lawyers in the form of Outlook-centric practice and document management, and clients will gain more access to their own case file information.

But with all those years of fits, starts, progress, steps back, steps forward in the developing legal technology world, and in spite of the title of this book, this is *not* fundamentally about technology, actually not at all. Huh? Have I lost my mind? How can a book with the title *The 2009 Solo and Small Firm Legal Technology Guide* not be about technology?

Simple.

It's about success. Successful law practice. Success in satisfying and retaining clients. Success in meeting and exceeding the competition. Success financially. Success in finding satisfaction in law practice and with oneself. Not about technology. Because technology, properly understood, properly selected and properly implemented, is merely an enabler—an enabler of all the aforementioned successes.

Lawyers are just beginning to realize that mere technology itself will not help them make more money, satisfy clients more thoroughly or help them succeed in law practice. Rather, it is now understood that only well-selected, well-implemented technology, integrated into the workflow of law practice, intertwined with case-handling procedures, are the things that matter. When legal technology is subsumed into the bigger picture of law practice management, workflow streamlining, and seen in its proper light of enabling ultimate client satisfaction, the age of legal technology enlightenment is upon us.

Few legal technologists yet "get" this concept: that legal technology is not about technology at all. Rather, it's about finding ways to practice more profitably, deliver higher quality services to clients, improve response time, allow a practice to be a more potent competitor in its market niche and geographical region, ease some of the aggravation of law practice, and—dare I say, it?—to even make law practice fun again.

Law practices and the consultants who guide them and who can see past the mere bits and bytes to this endgame perspective will benefit dramatically. Again, few get these concepts. Our authors, Sharon D. Nelson, John W. Simek and Michael C. Maschke, are some of the few who do. So read on and know that while you're reading about the technology you'll use in your practice, you're really reading about how you and your clients can achieve the ultimate in win-win professional relationship success.

CHAPTER ONE

Computers

Desktop Computers

Personal Computers (PCs)

The Dell OptiPlex line of computers offers the perfect combination of performance and business-grade hardware, business computing without compromise—and at the right price. Dell computers can be purchased with a three-year or four-year warranty, and offer a large selection of available warranty options when it comes to protecting your investment. They offer both hardware and software warranty protection, along with same-day or next-business day response for the replacement of failed computer hardware or software. For the added premium, purchasing software technical support, in our judgment, is generally not worth the additional cost.

Below, we provide you with our recommendations for a Dell OptiPlex business-grade system with all of the hardware components included:

Computer Model:	Dell OptiPlex 755 Mini-Tower Computer
Operating System:	Microsoft Windows XP Professional
Processor:	Intel Core 2 Duo 3.16 GHz
Memory:	2-GB DDR2 667MHz
Video Card:	Intel GMA3100
Hard Drive:	160-GB SATA 3.0GB/s with 8-MB DataBurst Cache
Optical Drive:	16X DVD+/-RW
Network:	Intel 82566DM Gigabit Ethernet LAN solution 10/100/1000
Warranty:	3-Year, Next Business Day, Onsite Parts and Labor
Other:	Vista Premium Downgrade Relationship Desktop 1394 FW Controller Card, PS2 Serial Port Adapter, 9 USB Ports, 305 Watt Power Supply

Dell OptiPlex 755
Model Line

The Intel Core 2 Duo 3.16-GHz processor will provide enough power to support both current and future versions of business-grade software throughout the life of the machine. The Intel Core 2 Duo has replaced the Intel Pentium 4 processor and is the standard for business-grade systems. Dell now includes the Intel Core 2 Quad processor as an available upgrade when configuring your OptiPlex computer, but at this point the upgrade isn't worth the added cost (~$300). The Intel Core 2 Duo processor is offered with varying levels of clock speed, with the 3.16-GHz version in the middle of the range of processer speeds that Dell currently offers. The faster the processor, the higher the premium you will pay for having cutting-edge technology. The amount of memory included in this system will be enough to support your business applications, handling even "memory-hungry" applications with ease. Two gigabytes (GB) of memory has become the de facto standard for the minimum amount of memory in business-grade computers, given the low cost and high gain in performance for the upgrade.

The video card included in this system allows for both Video Graphics Array (VGA) and Digital Visual Interface (DVI) outputs. With both interfaces available to choose from, you can be more selective when purchasing a monitor for your system. Monitors, keyboards, and other peripherals are discussed in a later section.

The hard drive plays an important role in the configuration of your computer system, because it is the component that stores your data. In short, the better the hard drive, the faster your computer can read and write your data. This system comes with a 160-GB Serial ATA (SATA) II hard drive, which will provide enough storage space for the average lawyer user. The SATA II (3.0 GB/s) interface is the latest generation of the Serial ATA specification, allowing for more throughput and higher cache than the previous SATA I (1.5 GB/s) specification. In fact, Dell no longer offers SATA I hard drives as an option in their OptiPlex desktop configuration.

The 16X DVD+/-RW Drive will allow you to burn both CDs and DVDs. The PS2 Serial Port adapter will allow your system to use older mice and keyboards instead of the more common USB-interfaced devices, as well as connect to legacy serial devices. The additional cost of approximately $10 makes this upgrade worthwhile. With the addition of the FireWire card adapter, external FireWire devices can be connected to and used on the system.

Now, on to the most important advice that we will give you about purchasing a new business-grade computer: **Do not purchase a computer with Microsoft Windows Vista.** That's it, plain and simple. The outcry over the problems that people have encountered with Microsoft's newest operating system have not gone unheard. Dell, along with other major computer manufacturers, is still selling business computer systems that come preinstalled with Microsoft Windows XP Professional. When selecting this configuration, you are actually purchasing a Microsoft Windows Vista license, but the computer ships preinstalled with Microsoft Windows XP Professional. If the time comes when you need to upgrade the operating system to Windows Vista, you can do so without having to purchase a new license.

The three-year, next-business-day onsite parts and labor warranty will cover system hardware defects and failures for three years. The warranty's cost is built into the system's overall price and is relatively small. Dell provides the consumer with a toll-free number for technical support; if the hardware needs to be replaced, Dell will send someone out with a new part by the next business day. The replacement and labor cost for the hardware is covered. The three-year warranty will provide you with coverage for the system's expected life cycle. The Dell OptiPlex 755 Mini-Tower desktop computer can be purchased from Dell's Web site starting at $1,100.

Remember that the "sweet spot" in buying computers changes regularly. Our specs will get you close, but they will shift slightly during the lifespan of this publication. You can receive a courtesy copy of our current specs by e-mailing **sensei@senseient.com** and simply making a request.

Apple Computers (Macs)

Apple Macintosh (or Mac) computers are still not as widely used in law offices as Windows-based computers, but are starting to be chosen more frequently by attorneys, since Apple shifted to using Intel-based processors in all of their systems. As a result of this change, Macs can now run both the Mac OS X and Windows operating systems on the same computer. In a way, it's like having two systems in one.

A Mac computer can easily be configured to connect to and function on a Windows-based network, including the ability to communicate and authenticate with a Windows Domain Controller. In the past, however, Macs were used primarily by businesses with a need for multimedia functions such as video editing and graphic design, both areas in which Apple systems excelled. Usually, Apple's appearance in an office environment was the result of someone having personal preference for the Macintosh operating system over Windows. For those concerned with computer security, Mac systems are more secure than their Windows-based counterparts, since they are not targeted as often due to the smaller number of

Mac users overall. The more succesful they become, the more unwelcome attention they will receive from those who write malware.

While it is still not very common, we are beginning to see Apple computers make their way into smaller law offices, especially in a solo stand-alone environment. Now that Apple computers use Intel chipsets, users are taking advantage of the opportunity to better integrate with the Windows world. Some users run Windows on their Macs as the primary operating system. Others use Boot Camp, a free utility provided by Apple with each system, to dual boot between Windows and the Mac OS. With Boot Camp, you can install a Microsoft Windows XP or Windows Vista operating system alongside Apple's OS X on any Intel-based Macintosh computer. Boot Camp guides users through the creation of a new partition on which to install the Windows operating system, as well as using the Mac OS X Leopard disc to install Windows drivers for all of the hardware.

Some users have even purchased products like Parallels Workstation, or downloaded VirtualBox, which allows you to run Windows, Linux and other operating systems within the Mac OS itself. Virtual Machine (VM) software is described in more detail in a later section.

The iMac desktop systems combine performance and ergonomics by putting the hardware components that make up the system in the same case as the monitor, eliminating the need for separate components. As a result, the space-saving design allows you to free up both desk and floor space, without giving up performance. Below, we provide you with our recommendation for an iMac business-grade desktop system with all of the hardware components included:

Computer Model:	20-inch iMac Computer
Processor:	Intel Core 2 Duo 2.66 GHz
Memory:	2-GB 800 MHz DDR2 SDRAM
Video Card:	256-MB ATI Radeon HD 2600 Pro Graphics Card
Hard Drive:	320-GB SATA 7200 RPM Hard Drive
CD/DVD-ROM:	8X SuperDrive (DVD+R DL/DVD±RW/CD-RW)
Network:	10/100/1000 Base-T Gigabit Ethernet Adapter, AirPort Extreme Wi-Fi wireless networking adapter (802.11a/b/g/draft-n), Bluetooth 2.1 + EDR
Other:	iSight Camera, built in 20-inch monitor and stereo speakers, 1 FireWire 400, 1 FireWire 800, 3 USB Ports, keyboard and mouse
Warranty:	3-Year AppleCare Protection Plan for iMacs

The 20-inch iMac computer comes standard with the Intel Core 2 Duo processor. The 2 GB of memory included in this system will be enough to support your legal applications, but if you are considering an iMac strictly for multimedia purposes, you may want to add memory. The 320-GB 7200-RPM SATA hard drive comes standard and will deliver more than enough storage space and hard drive performance for the average lawyer. However, if you feel that you need additional storage space, the hard drive can be upgraded to 500 or 750 GB.

20-Inch iMac Computer

The standard Ethernet adapter and AirPort wireless adapter will allow your computer to connect to the business network, even if it's Windows-based. The AirPort wireless adapter is based on the Institute of Electrical and Electronics Engineers (IEEE) 802.11n draft specification and is backwards compatible with 802.11a/b/g wireless networks. If the 802.11n draft amendment is approved and becomes a standard, no further hardware upgrades to the system will be needed, since the Airport wireless adapter is already 802.11n compatible.

The other standard hardware included with the iMac is a built-in camera (iSight), stereo speakers, 20-inch monitor, one FireWire 400, one FireWire 800, and three USB ports. The system also includes the standard Apple keyboard and Mighty Mouse. The 20-inch iMac computer weighs 20 pounds and has a depth of about 7.5 inches, making it very easy to install one of these systems on your desk.

Apple's standard warranty with a new iMac provides you with 90 days of telephone support and one year of service coverage. We recommend that you upgrade the warranty to the extended AppleCare Protection Plan for iMacs, which provides you with telephone and service support for three years. Extending the warranty plan costs $169 and is well worth it. The 20-inch iMac computer can be purchased from Apple's online store for $1,499.

Laptops

Personal Computers (PCs)

The Dell Latitude line of laptop computers continues to combine performance and mobility in a laptop system that cannot be beat. These laptops are thin and very lightweight, weighing under five pounds. They are a perfect fit for the mobile lawyer and provide an ideal computing solution when you're on the go. Below, we provide you with our recommen-dations for a Dell Latitude business-grade laptop with all of the hardware components included:

Computer Model:	Dell Latitude E6400
Processor:	Intel Core 2 Duo 2.53 GHz
Operating System:	Genuine Windows Vista Business Bonus-Windows XP Professional downgrade
Memory:	2-GB DDR2 667 MHz SDRAM
Video Card:	NVIDIA Quadro NVS 160M with PC-Card
Hard Drive:	160-GB 7200 RPM Hard Drive (Free Fall Sensor)
CD/DVD-ROM:	8X DVD+/-RW Drive
Network:	10/100/1000 Mbps Ethernet Adapter, Intel WiFi Link 5100 802.11a/b/g/draft-n Mini Card, Internal Modem
Other:	14.1-Inch Wide Screen WXGA LCD Screen, 90W AC Power Adapter, 9 Cell/85 WHr Primary Battery, Weighs 4.37 Pounds, 4 USB 2.0 Ports, Integrated Webcam with Digital Microphone, Internal Finger-print Reader
Warranty:	3-Year, Next Business Day, Onsite Parts and Labor

Dell Latitude E6400 Laptop

The Dell Latitude E6400 comes with an Intel Core 2 Duo 2.53 GHz processor and 2 GB of memory, which should be sufficient to run all of the business applications of a mobile attor-ney. The system comes preinstalled with Microsoft Windows XP Professional, but also includes a license for Windows Vista Business. This allows the operating system to be upgraded to Vista at a later date, if necessary.

The system's fingerprint reader provides the level of security needed to protect your files and confidential data. If enabled, you can restrict user logon access to either the biometric access or a password. Protected by this fingerprint technology, data on the hard drive remains secure through encryption; that is, the hardware requires successful authentica-tion before the data contents of the hard drive can be decrypted.

The NVIDIA Quadro NVSvideo card supplies crisp, clear graphics to the 14.1-inch wide LCD display. The 160-GB hard drive will provide more than enough storage space for the mobile user, with a hard drive speed that will supply a faster disk performance. The DVD+/-RW drive will allow you to burn both CDs and DVDs. The Ethernet adapter will allow you to connect your laptop to your network when you're in the office, and the wireless network adapter will allow you to stay connected when on the move. The Intel wireless adapter provides connectivity to 802.11a/b/g and draft-n wireless networks, supporting dual band operation (2.4 and 5GHz) with data rates up to 300 Mbps. The nine-cell battery is an upgrade that can supply the laptop with power longer than the standard battery. It is a "must have" if you plan to use the wireless network adapter when running the laptop off the battery, although this will add a small amount of weight. The nine-cell battery will provide you with approximately three hours more battery life than the standard six-cell battery. Finally, the integrated Webcam with digital microphone is great for video conferences or recording audio.

The three-year, next business day onsite parts and labor warranty is the same one offered by Dell and described above in the Desktop Computers section. The Dell Latitude E6400 can be purchased from Dell's Web site starting at around $1,600.

If you are particularly clumsy or accident-prone, you may want to consider adding the CompleteCare Accidental Damage Protection Plan to your purchase. This plan covers any damage to the laptop, including such mishaps as liquid spills and dropping the device. Obviously, it does not cover intentional damage, theft and normal wear and tear. For the additional $150, you will have peace of mind when you set your coffee cup on the keyboard.

Apple Computers (Macs)

The Apple MacBook is perfect for the mobile attorney who needs a powerful notebook in a compact design. The MacBook laptop comes standard with the Intel Core 2 Duo processor, wide-screen display, built-in iSight camera, wireless adapter, and much more. The MacBook laptop is available only in the 13-inch model, with the 15-inch and 17-inch screens available on the MacBook Pro laptops.

The MacBook can be purchased in either white or aluminum colors, with the aluminum option starting at an additional $300. MacBooks can be fully integrated into any Windows-based network without too much overhead and configuration. Below, we provide our recommendations for an Apple MacBook business-grade laptop with all of the hardware components included:

Computer Model:	13-inch White MacBook
Operating System:	Mac OS v10.5 Leopard
Processor:	Intel Core 2 Duo 2.10 GHz
Memory:	2-GB 667 MHz DDR2 SDRAM
Video Card:	Intel GMA x3100
Hard Drive:	160-GB 5400 RPM SATA Hard Drive
CD/DVD-ROM:	8X SuperDrive (DVD+R DL/DVD±RW/CD-RW)
Network:	10/100/1000 Base-T Gigabit Ethernet Adapter, AirPort Extreme Wi-Fi wireless networking adapter (802.11a/b/g/draft-n), Bluetooth 2.1 + EDR
Other:	iSight Camera, 13.3-Inch Glossy Wide Screen Display, 60W MagSafe Power Adapter with cable management system, 55-watt-hour lithium-polymer battery, 2-USB 2.0 Ports, 1-FireWire 400 Port
Warranty:	3-Year AppleCare Protection Plan for MacBooks

13-Inch White MacBook Laptop

The 13-Inch MacBook laptop comes with an Intel Core 2 Duo 2.40 GHz processor, 2 GB of memory and the Mac OS v10.5 Leopard operating system. The Intel Integrated Graphics Media Accelerator video card provides perfect, high resolution to the 13.3-inch wide screen LCD display with a native resolution of 1280 x 800. The 160-GB hard drive provides enough space to store all or your documents, pictures, and music. The 8X SuperDrive will allow you to burn and play both CDs and DVDs. The built-in AirPort Extreme Wi-Fi adapter will keep you connected on the road and currently supports the 802.11n draft standard. The AirPort Extreme Wi-Fi adapter is backwards compatible with 802.11a/b/g wireless networks. The MacBook is also very light, weighing a total of just five pounds.

The solid-state scrolling trackpad gives you precise cursor control, supports two-finger scrolling, tap, double-tap, and drag capabilities. If you have been a lifelong Windows user, be forewarned: There is no right-click button on the trackpad. To right-click on a Mac, you must hold down the Control key while clicking.

Ever trip over a power cord and have your laptop come flying off the desk? With the 60W MagSafe Power Adapter, you no longer have to worry. The magnetic power connector will cleanly disengage from the side of the lap-top and cause no damage to the computer or the power cord. This a great gift to those of us who are occasionally less than graceful.

The sleek and elegant design of the MacBook is what sets it apart from the competition. Along with these qualities, the celebrated ease of use makes the MacBook a smart choice when purchasing a laptop for yourself or your firm. The MacBook can be purchased from Apple's online store start-ing at $1,100.

Computer Operating Systems

Microsoft Windows 98 and Windows 98 Second Edition Operating System

Microsoft Windows 98 and Microsoft Windows 98 Second Edition operat-ing systems have transitioned into an unsupported status with Microsoft. Since July 11, 2006, Microsoft has not provided any incident support options or security options. All versions of the Microsoft Windows 98 operating systems should be considered a security risk, and their use in business network environments should be discontinued—immediately!

Microsoft Windows 2000 Operating System

Microsoft Windows 2000 operating system was released in February 2000, and was made available in four editions: Professional, Server, Advanced Server and Datacenter Server. Microsoft Windows 2000 Professional Edi-tion was designed as the desktop operating system for businesses and offered greater security and stability than previous editions of the Win-dows desktop operating systems. The Microsoft Windows 2000 operating systems have transitioned into an extended support period until June 2010. During this time, Microsoft will provide security hot fixes and paid support but will no longer offer complimentary support, support options and nonsecurity hot fixes. It is still common to see Windows 2000 operat-ing systems being used in business networks, but plans should be made to phase out or upgrade machines running this operating system. Newly purchased computers don't come preinstalled with this version of the Microsoft Windows operating system.

Microsoft Windows XP Operating System

Microsoft Windows XP operating system was released in October 2001 and was made available in several editions: Professional, Home and the less common Media Center. Microsoft Windows XP Home was the first consumer-oriented operating system labeled as more "user friendly" than previous versions of Microsoft's operating systems. Windows XP Professional Edition was specifically designed for businesses and power users with added functionality and security. Currently, some estimates state that 90 percent of all business computers are running Windows XP Professional Edition.

Microsoft released Service Pack 3 for Windows XP in May 2008, with many industry insiders believing that this will be the last service pack developed for the operating system, which is about to enter extended support. In April 2009, Microsoft Windows XP will enter the extended support period before being phased out by 2014.

With the release of Microsoft Vista, direct OEM and retail sales of Windows XP have been discontinued as of June 2008. However, it is still possible to obtain computers preinstalled with Windows XP from system builders such as Dell, or by purchasing Windows Vista Ultimate or Business and then "downgrading" to Windows XP. Microsot Windows XP is still the operating system of choice when purchasing a new computer—at least until there is stability in Vista and until all legal applications will reliably run on Vista.

Microsoft Windows Vista Operating System

Microsoft Windows Vista operating system was released in January 2007 and was made available in six editions, with two editions designed for the business community. The editions released for this group are Windows Vista Business Edition and Windows Vista Enterprise Edition. Windows Vista Business Edition includes several new business features, such as file system encryption, full version of Remote Desktop, system image backup and recovery, Windows ShadowCopy, and the IIS Web server.

Early on, it was believed that Windows Vista Business Edition eventually would replace Microsoft XP Professional Edition as the dominant player in the business desktop operating system market, but this certainly has not been the case. Many companies are hesitant to upgrade their business systems because of Vista's continuning problems with incompatibility with some third-party software, licensing restrictions and costs, digital rights managements, driver issues for some peripherals, and the hardware requirements necessary to run the operating system.

In fact, there have been studies (by Devil Mountain Software, based in Florida) that document Vista operating notably slower than XP. The performance tests show Vista taking twice as long to execute some operations. To be fair, these tests were performed prior to the release of service packs and the latest patches, which have helped improve the performance issues. If you are purchasing new systems in 2009, make sure you check with your IT support person—and, for doggone sure, make certain that all of the software and peripherals you are running will work under Vista. Sometimes, the cost of replacing machines is greater than you might think because you are compelled to buy upgraded versions of your software, or other devices, so that your applications will run on the new system.

If you can hold out, Windows 7, the successor to Windows Vista, is just around the corner. In fact, rumors are that we should have a beta version of Windows 7 by the time this book is printed. As consumers, we can only hope that Redmond gets it right this time!

Microsoft Windows 7 Operating System

Windows 7 is the working name for the next major version of Microsoft Windows, the successor to Windows Vista. Microsoft has fast-tracked the development of this operating system, setting the expected release date for late 2009 or first quarter 2010. It is believed that Windows 7, will be more "XP-like," focusing on performance improvements and eliminating the compatability issues that have continued to plague Microsoft Vista. Will this be the operating system to get Redmond back on track? Only time will tell, so stay tuned. . .

Mac OS X version 10.5 (Leopard) Operating System

Mac OS X version 10.5 is the latest operating system released by Apple to come preinstalled on all newly purchased Macintosh computers. Mac OS X version 10.5 was released on October 26, 2007, and has since become a staple of the Apple movement to gain a greater market share of personal and business computers, with 20 percent of all Macs currently running the newest version of the Mac OS. The Mac OS X version 10.5 operating system is commonly referred to as "Leopard" and includes a number of new features intended to make the operating system more stable and reliable than Apple's previous operating systems. Leopard supports both PowerPC and Intel x86-based Macintosh computers. The Leopard operating system includes more than 300 changes and enhancements including a revised desktop, an updated Finder, Time Machine, Spaces, BootCamp preinstalled, and full support for 64-bit applications. A Single User license can be purchased for $129 and a Family Pack (five licenses) for $199 online from the AppleStore.

Mac OS X version 10.6 (Snow Leopard) Operating System

Mac OS X version 10.6 is currently in development and is planned to succeed the Leopard operating system. The new operating system is scheduled for release during third quarter 2009, and it is believed that Snow Leopard will focus primarily on performance improvements and overall efficiency of the operating system. One feature currently generating a lot of buzz is the inclusion of native support for connecting to Microsoft Exchange servers using the Address Book, Mail and iCal programs. Currently, users must purchase Microsoft Office for Macs and use Entourage for e-mail in a Microsoft Exchange environment. By adding native support for Microsoft Exchange servers, Apple may be able to gain a greater share of the business computing market.

CHAPTER TWO

Monitors

NOW THAT YOU HAVE your brand new desktop or laptop system with a docking station, you are ready for the task of picking out that brand new monitor—one that's big enough so you can actually see what you're doing! The days of 14-inch and even 15-inch monitors are long gone. You might even be able to reclaim some territory on your desk—and actually see some wood for a change. Just like computers, monitors come in all varieties, shapes, and sizes, and if you don't know what you're looking for, you can be inundated with all of the technical jargon that advertisers use to get you to purchase their monitors. Ever wondered what a HD LCD Wide-Screen with DVI, VGA, and HDMI inputs monitor is? We will explain how to weed through all of the technical jargon and will provide you with solid recommendations below for purchasing CRT, flat-panel LCD, Wide-Screen, and HD monitors.

CRT Monitors

The outdated technology, Cathode Ray Tube (CRT) monitors, are still around, believe it or not. You can still purchase them online, but generally they are no longer offered as an option when purchasing a new computer. Plus, why would you want to purchase a monitor that will take up half of your desktop space, generate a ton of heat and weigh 40 pounds? Although there still are reasons to have a CRT monitor, they are few and far between. First, for the most part they are still less expensive than their equivalent flat-panel monitor, which may be enough of a budgetary reason for someone to purchase one. However, shipping costs can eat up the savings because of the monitor's weight. We recommend that you pur-

Dell E773c
17-Inch Monitor

chase at least a 17-inch monitor, with a warranty. The CRT monitor that we recommend is the Dell E773c 17-inch color monitor. This model displays sharp and brilliant images at a maximum resolution of 1024 x 768 pixels, meaning that the monitor supports 1024 horizontal pixels ("dots") and 768 vertical ones. The monitor is black in color and, with its antiglare coating, all but ensures flicker-free images and easy viewing. The E773c can be purchased online at Dell's Web site for $149 and comes with a standard three-year warranty.

Flat Panel LCD Monitors

Flat panel monitors have all but taken over the computer monitor marketplace, essentially putting an end to the market for CRT monitors. The flat panel Liquid Crystal Display (LCD) monitors have a flat viewing screen that provides for a better viewing angle than CRT monitors. They are also less bulky in size, taking up only a fraction of the desktop space. Flat panel monitors have come down significantly in price over the past few years, and should be seriously considered as an alternative when purchasing a monitor for your computer system.

Flat panel monitors come in all different sizes, resolutions and performance. The flat panel monitor that we recommend is the Dell UltraSharp 1908FP 19-inch flat panel LCD monitor. This black monitor offers a resolution of 1280 x 1024 for sharp and brilliant images, an 800:1 contrast ratio for high color accuracy, and a 160-degree viewing angle. The monitor comes bundled with a height-adjustable stand, VGA/ DVI and USB cables, and it weighs only 12 pounds.

The Ultrasharp 1908FP comes with 4 USB 2.0 ports, making it easier to connect peripheral devices. The monitor also comes standard with a three-year hardware warranty. The Dell UltraSharp 1908FP 19-inch flat panel LCD monitor can be purchased online from Dell's Web site for $289.

Dell UltraSharp
1908FP 19-Inch Flat
Panel LCD Monitor

Widescreen Monitors

A step above LCD flat panel monitors, widescreen monitors offer higher resolutions, faster response times and have hit a nice sweet spot when it comes to the price. Widescreen monitors start at 19 inches and go upwards of 30 plus inches in width. Of course, the bigger the screen, the more you must be willing to pay.

The widescreen monitor that we recommend is a great compromise in size and value—the Dell E228WFP 22-inch widescreen monitor. This model offers a maximum resolution of 1680 x 1050, which will provide you with so much desktop real estate that you won't know what to do with it all. The high resolution lets you view documents, images, and videos with stunning detail, vivid colors, and seamless motion. The monitor offers the standard VGA, and Digital Video Interface (DVI) inputs, and can even be wall mounted. The Dell E228WFP 22-inch widescreen monitor can be purchased online from Dell's Web site for $249.

Dell E228WFP 22-Inch
Widescreen LCD Monitor

High-Definition Monitors

Just like high-definition (HD) televisions, HD monitors have come down in price as the competition has increased. Currently, there are a few vendors who make HD monitors that are reasonable in price. You can find HD monitors in all shapes, sizes, and price range, with some designed for the avid gamer and others for the multimedia guru. All HD monitors are going to require special graphics cards to utilize the brilliant HD display. The HD monitor that we recommend is the Dell UltraSharp 3007WFP-HC. The Dell 30-inch widescreen HD monitor is considered a visual wonder, sporting a high resolution of 2560 x 1600 that offers a brilliant, clear, and bright HD display. To fully utilize the ultra-high resolution settings, your computer must have a dual-link DVI-D graphics card that supports the 2560 x 1600 resolution.

Dell UltraSharp 3007WFP-HC
HD Monitor

The monitor supports EDTV (Enhanced Definition TV) and HDTV resolutions of 720p, 1080i and 1080p, which are defined standards. The monitor has a contrast ratio of 1,000:1, a 178-degree viewing angle, 4 USB 2.0 ports and a built-in 9-in-2 media card reader. This monitor is perfect for multimedia design, viewing HD movies or pictures, or for the individual who wants the best resolution. This monitor weighs 35 pounds and can be mounted on the provided stand or on the wall. The Dell UltraSharp 3007WFP-HC can be purchased online from Dell's Web site for $1,399, but it is frequently discounted up to $350. At this price, not only does it cost hundreds of dollars less than its competition, but its technical specifications are as good, if not better than, comparable models from other vendors.

Even though the cost is reasonable for a large wide screen monitor, you may want to consider using dual 19" or better monitors to get the equivalent surface area. Of course, your computer must have dual monitor support, which most of the newer computers have by default. You will find that purchasing dual monitors will be cheaper than one large one. And anecdotally, we have found that folks who move to dual monitors never want to go back!

CHAPTER THREE

Computer
Peripherals

IF YOU THOUGHT PURCHASING the right computer was tough, wait until you realize how many options there are when it comes to selecting computer peripherals! Having the right computer peripherals can make your computing experience faster, comfortable, and a better overall experience. Wireless devices have brought peripherals into a new dimension, getting rid of that Gordian knot wire mess that we all used to struggle to untangle. Below, we provide recommendations for mice, keyboards, wireless desktops, external storage devices and speakers.

Mouse

The optical mouse has brought the classic "roller ball" mouse to near extinction. Optical technology allows you to navigate with better speed, precision, and reliability. An optical mouse uses Light Emitting Diode (LED) technology that bounces light off of a surface onto a sensor. It is important to note that the surface needs some texture to work properly. It won't work on glass, for instance. The sensor analyzes the patterns in the images and compares them with previous captured images to determine how far the mouse has moved and relays the coordinates to the computer. It is really quite a scientific marvel. An optical mouse contains no moving parts and therefore doesn't require the maintenance and cleaning that a legacy roller ball mouse does. They even work without having to use the dreaded mouse pad.

Our recommendation for an optical mouse is the Microsoft IntelliMouse Explorer. This optical mouse provides advanced performance, ergonomic design, and customizable buttons. As an example, one button can be pro-

Microsoft Intelli-
Mouse Explorer

grammed for "delete" and one can be defined as the "back" button for your browser. The tilt-wheel technology allows you to scroll four ways (up, down, left, and right), allowing you to navigate long documents with ease. The Microsoft IntelliMouse Explorer sells for around $30 and can be purchased from your local electronics retailer. You also may want to consider the excellent Microsoft Notebook mouse for those users who travel with laptops and want a nifty little Bluetooth travel mouse.

Keyboards

Finding the right keyboard for your computer can be a tedious task, as you sift through all of the different keyboards and features to find one that you really want. When selecting a keyboard, you want to choose one that is ergonomically designed so that stress placed on your wrists is minimized. Second, you shouldn't have to give up comfort in order to gain enhanced features such as My Favorites buttons or buttons that will adjust the volume level of your speakers.

The keyboard we recommend is the Natural Ergonomic Keyboard 4000 from Microsoft. This keyboard is a great blend of ergonomic design and functionality. The reverse slope keyboard has a cushioned palm rest that allows you to rest your wrists and hands when typing, and provides greater comfort. The customizable My Favorites Keys allow you to open your most frequently used software, pictures, videos, and music. You can even browse the Internet with the push of a button. The MultiMedia Keys allow you to control your media player from your keyboard, along with the volume level of your speakers. This keyboard connects to your computer through the USB interface and comes with software to help you customize your keyboard's features. The Natural Ergonomic Keyboard 4000 from Microsoft can be purchased for around $30 from your local electronics retailer.

Natural Ergonomic
Keyboard 4000
from Microsoft

Wireless Keyboard Desktops

With the introduction of wireless technology, wireless keyboard desktops have become extremely popular. A wireless keyboard desktop is a keyboard and mouse desktop combination that connects to your desktop computer wirelessly using Radio Frequency (RF) technology. The keyboard and mouse are powered with standard or rechargeable batteries and transmit their signals to a desktop receiver that is connected to the computer. It requires very little set-up to install, and eliminates the need for cables, which have plagued computer users since the first PC came into existence.

Our recommendation for purchasing a wireless keyboard desktop is the Logitech Cordless Desktop Wave Pro system. This wireless keyboard desktop comes with a wave key design that provides superior comfort with full size, full travel keys designed for quiet operation. The slight constant curve of the keyboard features consistently sized keys that let you type with confidence and ease. The keyboard uses the standard QWERTY arrangement, so you don't have to relearn how to type, as you do with other curved keyboards. The height of the keyboard is adjustable, allowing you to choose what's most comfortable for you. The model uses 128-bit AES encryption to secure data as it's transmitted from the keyboard to the receiver.

The Rechargeable MX 1100 Cordless Laser Mouse is rechargeable through a USB cradle, and operates up to two months on a full charge. The laser mouse uses a small infrared laser instead of an LED, which increases the resolution and sensitivity of the mouse.
This system is Microsoft Vista compatible. The Logitech Cordless Desktop Wave Pro system can be purchased for around $130 from your local electronic retailer or online at **www.logitech.com**.

Logitech Cordless Desktop Wave Pro

External Storage Devices

External storage devices are devices that connect to your computer via the USB or FireWire interfaces to store electronic data. These devices come in all sizes, shapes, colors, and volume of storage space. They have all but replaced the CD-ROM and DVD as the leading means to store electronic data, because of their portability, low cost, and vast amount of storage space. Be sure to consider some type of secure authentication or encryption for external storage, especially if confidential client information is backed up or stored on the devices.

External Hard Drives

External hard drives are great locations to store videos, pictures, and music or to back up the data from your internal hard drive. The devices are easy to install and use. Most external hard drives are plug and play, which means you simply just have to plug them in to use them. How easy is that? External hard drives are not as fast as internal hard drives, but they are relatively inexpensive to buy and for the volume of data they can store, are a very good backup solution. Also, lawyers who are otherwise technically challenged seem to do well with this form of backup, which can really be reduced to the push-of-a-button method that so many attorneys seem to prefer.

The Maxtor OneTouch 4 external hard drive is the perfect external storage solution, even for most technology illiterate computer users. The Maxtor OneTouch 4 model comes with available capacities of 320, 500 and 750 GB, and one terabyte (TB) of storage space. These capacities provide you with flexibility that allows you to select the amount of desired storage space that best meets your needs. The Maxtor OneTouch button located on the external hard drive communicates with backup software installed on your computer to begin the backup process with the touch of a button. Each model should provide enough storage space to back up all of the data required by most attorneys with ease. The device connects to your computer through the USB 2.0 interface and is hot-swappable,

meaning you don't have to power down for disconnection. The drive is whisper quiet and can sit on your desk or computer without taking away valuable space. This external hard drive is compatible with Macs and Windows alike. The Maxtor OneTouch 4 external hard drive can be purchased online at **www.maxtor.com** for between $99 and $230, depending on storage capacity.

Maxtor OneTouch 4
External Hard Drive

Thumb Drives

USB thumb drives (aka flash drives) are small, portable storage devices that use flash memory to store electronic data. Currently, they are offered with storage volume sizes ranging from 32 MB to 64 GB. For the most part, USB thumb drives with capacities of 512 MB and smaller have been largely discontinued. USB thumb drives offer many advantages over other portable storage devices such as the floppy disk, CD-ROM and DVD. In particular, they are smaller, more durable, faster, and can hold more data. Unfortunately, these devices create a great security risk for small businesses and law firms because their small size makes them absurdly easy to lose. This risk can be minimized, however, by purchasing the SanDisk Extreme Cruzer Contour USB thumb drive.

The SanDisk Extreme Cruzer Contour USB thumb drive is available with storage capacities of 4, 8, and 16 GB of storage space for your files, and comes standard with AES hardware encryption to keep your data secure. The USB thumb drive includes U3 technology, so you can carry your files and software on a secure drive. U3 smart drives differ from traditional USB thumb drives because they come preinstalled with the U3 Launch-pad, a program that launches upon insertion of the device. The Launch-pad can be configured to require a password to be entered before access to the data partition of the hardware is granted. This secure authentication protects your data in the event that the USB thumb drive is lost or stolen. The authentication process only takes a few seconds, so it is not overly taxing—and what price would you put on keeping your client data confidential? U3 applications can be installed and run directly from the USB thumb drive, without leaving any remnant data on the host system. As an added security precaution, entering an invalid password too many times will result in the USB thumb drive becoming unusable, requiring a reformat of the device before it can be used again.

The device is compatible with the Microsoft Windows 2000 Service Pack 4, Microsoft Windows XP, Microsoft Vista and Mac OS X v.10.1.2+ operating systems. The SanDisk Extreme Cruzer Contour USB thumb drive can be purchased online at **www.sandisk.com** for between $59.99 and $149.99, depending on the storage capacity.

SanDisk Extreme Cruzer Contour USB Thumb Drive

Another excellent choice is the 4-GB Basic Secure Flash Drive from Iron-Key (**www.ironkey.com**), which also comes in 1-, 2-, and 8-GB versions. This USB device is designed for the needs of sensitive military, government, and enterprise networks, and includes AES hardware encryption that has been validated to meet government Federal Information Processing Standard (FIPS) requirements. The security features require no software or drivers to enforce, with all the security being handled by the device hardware. The device requires a user to authenticate with a password before encryption keys are enabled and data can be accessed. This device is even waterproof! Good for those of us who are constantly running our USB thumb drive through the washer.

This device has a self-destruct mechanism (think *Mission Impossible*) that will wipe the data contents if a user or thief tries to break into the IronKey and enters 10 incorrect passwords. Another included application is the Password Manager and Password Generator. The Password

Generator application will generate very secure passwords of whatever length you desire. The Password Manager securely stores your passwords on the IronKey along with the associated Web address. Merely insert your IronKey device in your computer and go to a Web site that requires a user ID and password. The IronKey will prompt you to save the credentials if it is the first time IronKey has "seen" the site. If the logon credentials are already stored on the IronKey, a dialog box will be presented to confirm if the ID and password should be retrieved from the secure Password Manager application. Make sure you back up your password

IronKey

"vault" to the IronKey site in case the IronKey is lost or damaged. The password information is backed up to IronKey in a secure encrypted fashion. If you ever lose your IronKey device, just restore your password information from the IronKey site.

FireWire Devices

FireWire devices are similar to their USB counterparts, except that they take advantage of the FireWire standard and offer transfer rates of up to 786 Mbps, often referred to as FireWire 800 devices. These gadgets are great for professional applications, digital audio/video, graphic design, and system backups. They are identical to other external hard drives, except for the additional FireWire 800 interface that they support.

The external LaCie Hard Disk, Design by Neil Poulton is an ultra-quiet hard drive in a sleek design that comes with enough storage capacity to meet your needs. This model boasts three different interfaces: USB 2.0, FireWire 400 and FireWire 800, to connect the device to your computer. It's available with storage capacities of 500 GB, 750 GB and 1 TB. When taking advantage of the FireWire 800 connection, you can transfer data up to 800 Mbps, or double the transfer rates of FireWire 400 devices. This device is both Mac and Windows compatible, requires very little set-up (just plug and play), and offers automatic formatting with LaCie Setup Assistant software. The LaCie '1-Click' backup software for both PCs and Macs is included for quickly saving important files in one click. The external LaCie Hard Disk, Design by Neil Poulton can be purchased online at **www.lacie.com** for between $139.99 and $229.99, depending on storage capacity, or from your local electronics retailer.

External LaCie Hard Disk,
Design by Neil Poultron

Speakers

Lawyers (and their staff) often tell us that the most important peripheral device they need for their computer is a pair of speakers. They like to be able to listen to their music while they work and are adamant about fidelity. Without breaking the bank, reasonable quality desktop speakers can be purchased to provide the user with a clear, true sound. Logitech, a leading provider in speaker systems for computers, makes the LS21 Speakers. The LS21 speakers offer 2.1 stereo sound with a subwoofer providing enhanced bass. The speakers come in a slim, stylish profile, offering quality

audio at a reasonable price. The speakers have a stereo headphone jack, an auxiliary input where you can connect your iPod or MP3 player, and integrated controls located on a wired remote. The Logitech LS21 speakers can be purchased online for around $30 from **www.logitech.com**.

Logitech LS21 Speakers

Be careful of speaker "wars" in the office as people battle for the loudest music. Headphones may be a consideration in providing a quieter office environment.

If you purchase one of the recommended Dell flat panel monitors, consider adding a sound bar. The sound bar clips on the bottom edge of the Dell flat panel and gets its power from the monitor itself. It provides a clean installation and doesn't take up any additional desk space.

CHAPTER FOUR

Printers

EVEN IN THE ERA of the "paperless office," most law firms still print a lot of documents on a daily basis, probably more than any other business. To say that the practice of law tends to be "less than green" is a massive understatement. Nonetheless, it is certainly critical to have a good, reliable printer to ensure that your firm is printing quality documents in the shortest amount of time. Below, we discuss and recommend printers for stand-alone systems, network systems, and multifunctional printers/copiers.

Stand-Alone Printers

Your most basic printer is the stand-alone printer. This printer connects directly to a computer and is not placed on the network. It only has to be capable of handling one user's print jobs at a time. Even when networked printers are used, there can be reasons to also have stand-alone printers—perhaps so the bookkeeper may keep financial records from inadvertently being left for someone else to pick up. Senior partners may feel their data is so confidential that they want a printer in their office (though their staff often mutters that they are just too lazy to walk down the hall). There are many makes and models to choose from when selecting a stand-alone printer, and each has different performance specifications, features, and available fonts.

Usually, the first question we get asked when recommending a stand-alone printer for a law firm or small business is, "Should I purchase an ink-based printer or a laser printer?" We highly recommend going with a laser printer. They are more economical in the long run versus ink jets. Ink jet printers typically result in a higher cost of ownership over the long haul, with ink cartridges printing at a higher cost per page than the average laser printer. There are even studies that show a cost of $3,000-$5,000 per gallon for name brand ink cartridges. Does that make you feel any better about the cost of gasoline?

The second question we are asked most often is, "Should I purchase a color or a black and white laser printer?" You will pay a premium for a color laser printer and in most instances it is not worth the cost when purchasing a stand-alone printer. It is usually more cost-effective to purchase a color laser printer to be placed on the computer network so that more than one user can print to it.

The Hewlett Packard (HP) LaserJet P1505 printer is the perfect solution for the stand-alone printer. This printer prints as many as 24 pages per minute, comes standard with a paper input capacity of 260 sheets, and has a recommended monthly volume of up to 2,000 pages. The printer has a first page out speed as fast as 6.5 seconds and supports all the common page types such as letter, legal, executive and envelopes. This printer comes standard with 2 MB of memory and connects to your computer using the USB interface. It should be noted that the printer doesn't come with a USB cable, which will have to be purchased separately.

This black and white printer was designed for quick business printing and offers a cost-effective solution to personal printing. The printer is both Mac and Windows compatible, including Vista. The HP LaserJet P1505 printer can be purchased online for around $149 from **www.hp.com**.

HP LaserJet P1505 Printer

Networked Printers

Networked printers are used to provide a printing resource to multiple users. They are generally installed in a central location and then shared throughout the local network. Administration and security of these printers can be integrated into your network's security infrastructure, such as Windows Active Directory, for a Windows-based network. Installation in a central location simplifies both management and security of these devices. The network printers can be shared out to the various computers that make up your network with very little overhead to complete the task.

There are many types of network printers and depending on your need—low-volume, high-volume, or color—your options will vary. A popular request from many law offices is multiple trays for the printer. Multiple-paper-type capability is usually restricted to the intermediate and higher-end printer models.

Low-Volume Network Printers

Low-volume network printers are printers designed for small to moderate print volume with an expected print volume as great as 5,000 pages per month. These printers are moderately priced and are primarily used to segment printing within offices based on user group or physical location. Network printers have more robust hardware than stand-alone printers to handle multiple jobs from different users at the same time.

The HP LaserJet P2015x black and white network-based laser printer is great for the small law firm, because it will provide your users with a highly reliable, cost-effective printer that will be capable of handling the amount of volume produced by these types of offices. The HP LaserJet P2015x prints as many as 27 pages per minute and has a monthly recommended volume of 3,000 pages. It comes standard with an input capacity of 500 sheets, 32 MB of memory, and it handles all sizes of paper. The printer features an embedded HP Jetdirect Fast Ethernet print server to attach the printer to your local network. It should be noted that the printer doesn't come with a USB or network cable, either of which will have to be purchased separately.

The paper input capacity and memory can be upgraded if desired, and the printer's drivers are compatible with both Mac and Windows-based systems, including Vista. The printer comes with a standard one-year warranty and includes a CD-ROM with the drivers and software necessary to configure the device. The HP LaserJet P2015x black and white laser printer can be purchased online for around $449 from **www.hp.com**.

HP LaserJet
P2015X Printer

High-Volume Network Printers

High-volume network printers are printers designed for businesses that need the capacity to print a large volume of pages on a monthly basis, and are usually considered when your firm needs a printer that can print more than 5,000 pages per month. These devices contain hardware that can handle the volume load and are built to be constantly printing.

The HP 9050n black and white network-based laser printer is ideal for firms that print large volumes of documents on a monthly basis. This printer has a recommended monthly printing volume of 15,000–50,000 pages, and prints up to 50 pages per minute. The printer comes with a standard input capacity of 1,100 sheets, three paper trays, 128 MB of memory, and an embedded HP Jetdirect Fast Ethernet print server to attach the printer to your local network. This printer accommodates all sizes of paper and can easily be upgraded with more memory, an optional hard drive, paper trays, or envelope feeders. The network connectivity can be upgraded to support wireless networks, a "must have" option for those firms that use a wireless infrastructure for their local network. It should be noted that the printer doesn't come with a USB or network cable, which will have to be purchased separately.

The printer comes with a one-year, next business day onsite warranty. The printer is compatible with both Mac and Windows-based networks, including Vista, and comes with a CD-ROM that contains both printer driver files and software necessary to manage and configure the device. The HP LaserJet 9050n printer can be purchased online for around $3,399 from **www.hp.com**.

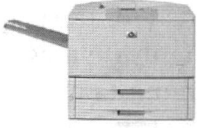

HP LaserJet
9050n Printer

Color Network Printer

Color network printers are essential for any law firm or small business that wants to print any significant volume of documents in color. By networking the color printer, multiple users can have access to the shared resource, which is far more cost-effective than giving everyone their own color printer. HP is still the leading manufacturer of color printers, in terms of value, selection, overall reliability, and performance. Their color LaserJet printers are reasonably priced and produce high-quality color documents.

For a small business or law firm, the HP Color LaserJet CP3505n printer is perfect for everyday color printing. This printer prints as many as 22 pages per minute for both black and color, has a recommended monthly volume of 1,500–5,000 pages, and a first page out speed of less than 12.5 seconds. The standard input capacity is 350 sheets of paper but that can be upgraded to 850 sheets. The printer supports all sizes of paper and can be upgraded with an envelope feeder.

The printer comes standard with 256 MB of memory and an embedded Jetdirect Fast Ethernet print server that enables the printer to connect to your local network. The printer's drivers support both Mac and Windows-based systems, including Vista, and can be networked for easy accessibility. The printer comes with a one-year, next-day and onsite limited warranty.

The HP Color LaserJet CP3505n printer can be purchased online for around $599 from **www.hp.com**. It should be noted that the printer doesn't come with a USB or network cable, either of which will have to be purchased separately.

The largest operational cost for a color laser printer is the consumables. Color cartridges are not cheap and color prints can be very expensive. Digital copier manufacturers are beginning to take over the space of color printing. Investigate using a color copier for your color print needs versus a stand-alone color printer. You might be surprised at the amount of money that could be saved.

HP Color LaserJet
CP3505n Printer

Multifunctional Printers/Copiers

Don't you wish there was a single device that you could install on your local network that could do everything your office needs every day—printing, faxing, scanning, and copying? Ask and ye shall receive. Multifunctional printers (MFPs) offer the capability to print, scan, copy, and fax from the same device, combining the functions of multiple devices into just one, and eliminating the need to purchase a separate scanner, copier, printer and fax machine. In the long run, purchasing or leasing an MFP can save you time and money expended to upgrade and service multiple devices. These devices are very expensive and are generally leased because of the high cost to purchase.

When deciding whether to buy or lease an MFP, there are some functionality questions that you want to keep in mind:

- ◆ Does the firm want the ability to print in both color and black and white?
- ◆ Do we need duplex printing?
- ◆ Do we want to scan documents to hard drive, user box, or e-mail?
- ◆ Do we want incoming faxes to be sent to e-mail as an image file or just printed?
- ◆ Do we want to be able to link the use of the MFP to the firm's billing program?

 ♦ What does our printing capacity need to be?

 ♦ Do we need any finishing capabilities?

 ♦ Do we need to implement any security on the unit, and if so, what types?

By answering these questions, you will be able to provide your vendors with enough detail to sell or lease you the MFP device that best meets the firm's needs. Your digital copier may already have some of these features installed, but not configured. Check with your vendor to see what capabilities your current copier has. In our office, we have a Konica Minolta Bizhub C250 MFP device. It allows us to print both in color and black and white at speeds up to 25 pages per minute; scan to hard drive, user box, or FTP; and fax documents, although we do not use that feature. We are able to download our scanned documents from a secure internal Web site as JPG, PDF or TIFF files. The Bizhub has advanced security features such as job erase, hard-drive sanitizing and lock, user authentication, IP address filtering, and secure print and scan encryption. Needless to say, the Bizhub provides us with a secure MFP option.

Konica Minolta Bizhub C250

As you work with your copier supplier, make sure you negotiate a low cost-per-color copy and only pay for the number of pages that you print. Don't pay for the consumables (e.g., toner cartridges) as these should all be included as part of the per-page cost.

CHAPTER FIVE

Scanners

ALMOST AS COMMON AS printers, scanners have become a necessary piece of equipment in most offices, as more paper documents are being scanned and stored electronically. The drive to a paperless office is still underway, but certainly there is steady progress in that direction. The setup and operation of scanners has become simple to a point that even the beginning computer user can do it. Many of the tasks that once had to be performed manually are now automated, and the hookup entails connecting a single wire and inserting a CD to install software. Network scanners may be a little more complex to set up and would require the assistance of the IT staff to configure.

Most desktop scanners communicate with the computer via the USB or FireWire interface and come with a variety of software to assist in the scanning and file conversion process. Some models come standard with Optical Character Recognition (OCR) software that will read the scanned image and produce a text document that is editable. Fujitsu, a manufacturer of home- and business-grade scanners, produces scanners that have been constantly rated the best models for businesses. Below, we make recommendations for both low-volume and high-volume scanners from Fujitsu.

Some law firms may already have scanning capability in their digital copier. As previously stated, check with your vendor to see if scanning with your copier is a more cost-effective solution than purchasing a stand-alone unit.

Low-Volume Scanner

For years, the Fujitsu ScanSnap has been the most recommended desktop scanner for attorneys. Given the size, specs and cost, you couldn't find a better deal. The small workhorse has provided users with the functionality commonly seen only in much bigger, more bulky pieces of equipment. The ScanSnap has been replaced by a new scanner from Fujitsu, an upgraded scanner on steroids.

The Fujitsu fi-6130 desktop scanner is touted as the fastest and most compact scanner in its class. This scanner takes up the same amount of desktop real estate as the ScanSnap S510, but scans documents more than twice as fast. The compact device scans documents at a rate of up to 40 pages per minute (grayscale) and comes with a 50-page auto-document feeder. Like many other Fujitsu scanners, this model comes bundled with Adobe Acrobat 8 Standard Edition and a one-year limited warranty. A one box scanning solution. Even the USB cable is included!

The scanner has a scanning resolution of 600 x 1,200 dpi and connects to the computer via the USB interface. The scanner is compatible with Microsoft Windows 2000 (SP 4)/XP (SP2)/Vista (32/64-bit) and Microsoft Windows Server 2003 (32/64-bit). The scanner comes with bundled software that includes Adobe Acrobat 8.0 Standard Edition, Kofax VRS Professional and ScandAll Pro.

Adobe Acrobat 8.0 Standard software allows you to automatically convert scanned data into searchable PDF files. Some of the automatic features of this device include enhanced hard embossed card scanning, and reversing

Fujitsu fi-6130
Scanner

roller technology providing unmatched reliability for a wide variety of document types and sizes. The scanner comes with a standard 1-year limited warranty that can be upgraded to the Advanced Exchange service program. The Fujitsu fi-6130 scanner can be purchased online from Fujitsu's web site (**www.fujitsu.com**) for around $850. The inclusion of Adobe Acrobat Standard (a $299 value) makes this a worthwhile purchase.

High-Volume Scanner

The Fujitsu fi-5530C2 is perfect for legal users who need a high-speed scanner on a modest budget. The built-in Automatic Document Feeder (ADF) holds 100 pages and scans up to 50 pages per minute in 200 dpi black and white mode. Everything needed for creating a paperless office is included free with the fi-5530C2, including Adobe Acrobat 8.0 Standard Edition, ScandAll Pro, and Kofax VRS Professional.

Using the Fujitsu fi-5530C2 scanner, you can convert any document to Adobe PDF using the Adobe Acrobat 8.0 Standard software that is included with the scanner. The scanner can withstand a vigorous duty cycle of up to 4,000 documents per day and can output paper ranging from business card size to a legal document. The Ultra SCSI and USB 2.0 interface allows for simplified connectivity to your computer.

Fujitsu
fi-5530C2 Scanner

The scanner is compatible with Microsoft Windows 2000/XP/Vista systems. The Fujitsu fi-5530C2 scanner can be purchased online from Fujitsu's Web site (**www.fujitsu.com**) for around $2,700.

This is a lot of money for a solo or small firm operation. We're sure that your digital copier could provide a less expensive solution for your scanning needs, especially if you have a newer unit.

CHAPTER SIX

Servers

ONE OF THE BIGGEST, most important and most expensive decisions that you will have to make regarding your firm's technology is when you have to purchase a server. This is the mothership of the network, and the purchase decision should be made very carefully.

Like workstations, servers come in every make, model, and flavor. Unlike workstations, however, servers can be very expensive and can consume a large chunk of your technology budget. Engage in careful planning when selecting a server, so that future needs can be discussed and addressed, including the desirable hardware and software components the server must have in order to meet your future goals. Think about today's needs, tomorrow's needs and your needs in four to five years, which is a server's average life span.

Solo—File and Printer Sharing

The most simple and basic reason for getting a server is for file and printer sharing. By centralizing the storage of electronic files, administration and installation of printers, you will save time, money, and headaches when it comes to maintaining and managing your network. There are servers designed specifically for the purpose of file and print sharing. These units come with the most basic hardware and software and are relatively inexpensive when compared with the mid-range to higher-end servers.

Dell PowerEdge 840 Server

The Dell PowerEdge 840 server was designed for the small business to provide the most basic file- and printer-sharing capabilities. Below, a listing of the server's hardware and software components and some technical specifications are provided:

Dell PowerEdge 840 Server

<u>Hardware Components</u>

Chassis:	Tower
Operating System:	Microsoft Windows Server 2003 R2 with SP2, Standard Edition with 5 CALs
Processors:	Quad Core Intel® Xeon® X3230, 2.66GHz, 8MB Ca
Memory:	4-GB DDR2 RAM
Primary Controller Card:	Perc 5/I SAS Internal RAID Adapter, PCI-Express Card
Hard Drive Configuration:	Add-in PERC5i (SATA/SAS) Controller which supports 3-4 Hard Drives—RAID-5
Hard Drives:	3—146 GB SAS, 3.5-Inch 15K RPM Hard Drives
CD/DVD Drive:	48X IDE CD-RW/DVD Combo Drive
Floppy Drive:	3.5-Inch 1.44 MB Floppy Disk Drive
Network Adapter:	Onboard Single Gigabit Network Adapter
Peripherals:	USB Mouse and Keyboard, 17-Inch Flat Panel Monitor
Warranty:	3-Year Basic Enterprise Support: 5x10 Hardware Only, 4 Hour 5x10 Onsite

The Dell PowerEdge 840 was customized through Dell's Web site (**www.dell.com**) and contains an Intel Quad Core Xeon 2.66-GHz processor with 4 GB of DDR2 RAM. The server comes with the Microsoft Windows Server 2003 R2 Standard Edition operating system with five Client Access Licenses (CALs). CALs are needed for each computer or user that accesses the server.

The 3 SAS (serial-attached SCSI) 146-GB hard drives are configured in RAID-5 (Redundant Array of Inexpensive Disks) for performance and fault-tolerance. In a RAID-5 hard drive configuration, if one of the hard drives were to fail, the server would continue to operate until the failed hard drive could be replaced. In most other hard drive configurations, if a server's hard drive fails, the server is inoperable until the disk is replaced. The RAID-5 configuration offers both fault-tolerance with the parity hard drive and better performance than most other RAID or mirrored disk configurations. The RAID-5 hard drive configuration is strongly recommended for all law firm servers.

In total, there is about 292 GB of space available for the storage of electronic data, programs, and other applications. You can save a little bit of money by reducing the disks and configuring for a RAID-1 (mirrored disks) arrangement. You will still get some fault tolerance with a RAID-1, but disk expansion is more costly and difficult. A RAID-5 configuration allows for easy expansion in the future.

The server comes with a USB mouse and keyboard, along with a 17-inch flat panel monitor. The onboard gigabit network adapter will allow clients to connect to the server at gigabit speeds, assuming the rest of the network components support such speeds. The CDRW/DVD drive will allow you to burn CD-ROMs from the server console, as well as read DVD discs. Although floppy disks have been replaced by CD-ROMs and DVDs, a floppy disk drive was included in the configuration of this server. Floppy disks are still used by Windows to install third-party drivers during the installation process and for emergency recovery disks. You don't want to be stuck in an emergency situation where you need to load drivers off of a floppy disk and can't get your server back online because it doesn't have a floppy drive.

One of the most important features to consider when purchasing a server is the warranty. In most cases, you will not need both hardware and software support. At a minimum, you must get a hardware warranty that will cover the hardware and labor cost to replace any failed components. The Dell PowerEdge comes with a three-year, four-hour, same-day onsite parts and labor warranty, which can be upgraded to a four-year warranty if desired. Having a warranty is critical to protecting your equipment and data. This is no time to emulate Ebenezer Scrooge. The Dell PowerEdge 840 server was quoted on Dell's Web site for approximately $3,500 when this book was written.

Small Firm—File and Printer Sharing/Hosting Services

When purchasing a server for your network, you must decide what function and role the server will play in your day-to-day operations. Besides file and printer sharing, it is common for small firms to host their company's e-mail. Although you can also host a Web site, we recommend that you outsource that to an ISP (Internet Service Provider) because of potential security issues. The added hosting services (e-mail and/or Web) will require a server with upgraded hardware to be able to provide the necessary resources for the services to operate reliably.

The Dell PowerEdge 2900 III was designed for small firms or businesses that are looking for a cost-effective solution to hosting their own e-mail or Web sites. The server's hardware and software components (and some technical specifications) are provided below:

Dell PowerEdge 2900 III Server

Dell PowerEdge 2900 III Server

Hardware Components

Chassis:	Tower
Operating System:	Microsoft Small Business Server 2003 R2 Standard Edition with SP2, Includes 5 CALs
Processors:	Dual Quad Core Intel Xeon Processors 2.33 GHz 1333MHz Front Side Bus
Memory:	4-GB DDR2 RAM
Primary Controller Card:	Perc 6/i Integrated Controller Card
Hard Drive Configuration:	Integrated SAS/SATA RAID-5
Hard Drives:	3–146 GB SAS, 3.5-Inch 15K RPM Hard Drives
CD/DVD Drive:	Combo CD-RW/DVD ROM Drive
Floppy Drive:	3.5-Inch 1.44 MB Floppy Disk Drive
Power Supply:	Redundant Power Supply with Y-Cord
Network Adapter:	Dual Embedded Broadcom NetXtreme II Gigabit Ethernet
Peripherals:	USB Mouse and Keyboard, 17-Inch Flat Panel Monitor
Warranty:	3-Year Basic Enterprise Support: 5x10 Hardware Only, 4 Hour 5x10 Onsite

The Dell PowerEdge 2900 III listed above was customized online through Dell. It contains Dual Quad Core Intel Xeon 2.33 GHz processors with 4 GB of DDR2 memory. The server specified above was customized in a tower chassis; however, the same model is available in a rack mount chassis for an additional $349. The rack mount chassis was designed for those firms and small businesses that maintain their servers and networking equipment in a rack. The processors will supply more than enough horsepower to configure the server as an e-mail or Web server, and the 4 GB of memory will allow these services to run smoothly.

The server comes with Microsoft Small Business Server 2003 (SBS) Standard Edition preinstalled, which includes the Microsoft Exchange 2003 Server software for e-mail hosting and IIS 6.0 for Web site hosting. Five CALs are also included, so you may have to budget for more if there are more than five devices in your firm accessing the server.

The 3-146 SAS 15K RPM hard drives are configured in a RAID-5 design, and provide about 292 GB of storage space for applications and data. The server comes with a USB mouse, keyboard, and a 17-inch flat panel monitor. Again, the PowerEdge server comes with the three-year Enterprise Basic Support warranty, which provides three years of four-hour, same-day parts and labor warranty. The Dell PowerEdge 2900 III server was quoted on Dell's Web site for approximately $3,700 when this book was written.

Don't forget to consider backup software and any additional (e.g., anti-virus, anti-spyware, anti-spam, etc.) software for the server.

Database/Applications Server

The software that your firm uses now and what it plans to use in the future will play a big role in determining what hardware and software components the server will need to adequately support your firm. So far, we have discussed the hardware and software specifications for a server used primarily for file and printer sharing, and a server capable of handling basic hosting services such as e-mail and a Web site. When planning to use a server to host a database application, case management, or e-discovery software, you must look at the minimum requirements for each piece of software and then go above and beyond the specifications that vendors will list. What vendors list should be regarded cautiously as a "bare minimum"—to run well and reliably, the software almost always requires more horsepower.

The recommended Dell PowerEdge 2900 server is capable of handling most database and software applications, as long as it's configured with an advanced hardware configuration to run the powerful applications. The server's hardware and software components are provided and described below:

Dell PowerEdge 2900 Server

Dell PowerEdge 2900 Server

Hardware Components

Chassis:	Tower
Operating System:	Microsoft Windows Server 2003 Enterprise Edition with SP2, Includes 25 CALs
Processors:	Dual Quad Core Intel Xeon Processors 2.83 GHz 1333MHz Front Side Bus
Memory:	8-GB DDR2 RAM
Primary Controller Card:	Perc 6/i Integrated Controller Card
Hard Drive Configuration:	Integrated SAS/SATA RAID-5
Hard Drives:	3–146 GB SAS, 3.5-Inch 15K RPM Hard Drives
CD/DVD Drive:	Combo CD-RW/DVD ROM Drive
Floppy Drive:	3.5-Inch 1.44 MB Floppy Disk Drive
Power Supply:	Redundant Power Supply with Y-Cord
Network Adapter:	Dual Embedded Broadcom NetXtreme II Gigabit Ethernet
Peripherals:	USB Mouse and Keyboard, 17-Inch Flat Panel Monitor
Warranty:	3-Year Basic Enterprise Support: 5x10 Hardware Only, 4 Hour 5x10 Onsite

The PowerEdge 2900 server described above was customized online through Dell and contains Dual Quad Core Intel Xeon 2.83 GHz processors and 8 GB of DDR2 memory. The processor included is faster (2.83 GHz) than the processor included with the server discussed in the hosting services section above.

The server comes with the Windows Server 2003 R2 Enterprise Edition operating system with Service Pack 2. The Windows Server 2003 R2 operating system does not come bundled with Microsoft Exchange Server or Microsoft SQL Server. However, Microsoft's SBS Premium does. So, if you want a single server to do "everything" such as file and print sharing, e-mail, and database hosting, SBS Premium may be a good alternative; but that's a lot of functionality to run on a single server and is not a generally recommended solution.

The three 146 GB hard drives are configured in a RAID-5 hard disk configuration and provide about 292 GB of storage space for applications and data. If more storage space is needed, this upgrade can be made during server configuration to meet your needs. The server comes with a USB mouse, keyboard, and 17-inch flat panel monitor.

The redundant power supply allows the server to stay powered on should one of the power supplies fail. The server comes with dual embedded Broadcom Ethernet adapters and a 48X CD-RW/DVD-ROM drive. The PowerEdge server comes with the three-year Enterprise Basic Support warranty, which provides three years of four-hour, same-day parts and labor warranty. The Dell PowerEdge 2900 server was quoted on Dell's Web site for approximately $7,300 when this book was written.

Virtual Servers

There is a large movement afoot to go to virtualization. This means that a single piece of hardware contains multiple server images. Virtualization enables the consolidation of data and applications onto a single hardware server. This saves energy, management, and administration effort, while reducing overall hardware and software costs, especially if your firm needs multiple servers. Virtualization is used for the separation of hosting services and applications, allowing for one virtual server to be down for maintenance without affecting the others. For example, if Windows updates were downloaded on a virtual server hosting File and Print Sharing services, the virtual server could be rebooted without having to bring down the entire host system, keeping other virtual servers online and available.

Virtualization is commonly used by larger firms and is not typically found in a small firm environment; however, we are recommending that more small firms begin considering virtualization technologies when making server hardware and software purchasing decisions.

Is server virtualization the best choice for your network environment? There are a number of questions that will need to be answered before making this determination.

First, what services and applications are running on your network? If your network is running Microsoft Exchange Server, SQL Server and a case management database, most likely you will need multiple servers to host all of these services and applications. Most case management applications now require a separate server to run on. By using virtualization, the purchase of another server can be avoided by installing the case management software on its own virtual server.

When purchasing a host system (the server hosting the virtual servers), the most critical hardware options that need to be considered are the amount of memory, number, and type of processors, and the amount of storage space. For each virtual server, 1 to 2 GB of memory will need to be allocated to provide the virtual server with enough memory resources to operate. This does not account for the 1 to 2 GB of memory that the host system will require as well. For example, if you have a host server running three virtual servers, you will need a minimum of 8 GB of memory installed in the host server to supply the host and all of the virtual servers with enough memory resources to operate. In order to accommodate the necessary hardware, the host system will have to be running Windows Server 2008 Enterprise Edition.

When running virtual servers, you will need to ensure that the host system has enough processing capability to manage the processing load. At a minimum, you'll want the system to contain Dual Core Intel Xeon processors with a processing speed of 2.5 to 3.33 GHz. The optimum solution is to use Quad Core Intel Xeon processors with the same speed range, and in virtualization solutions, you will need to have multiple processors. The multi-core processors combine two or more cores onto a single integrated circuit, providing multiprocessing capabilities to the chip. Multiprocessing allows the execution of multiple concurrent software processes in a system, which is vital in a virtualization solution.

The amount of storage space that will be required to run all of the virtual servers and the host system will vary from solution to solution. When determining the amount of storage space the systems will require, you will need to consider the services and applications that will be hosted. For example, a virtual server hosting Microsoft Exchange Server will require enough disk space to account for the size of both the Public and Private Exchange Database stores, along with the program files and operating system. The amount of storage space allocated to each virtual server can be independently configured and modified later if more space is needed. For ease of configuration and set up, bearing the cost of adding additional hard drive storage upfront makes more sense than waiting to add hard drives later on. Plus, it's always recommended to have more than enough hard drive space available to the host system and virtual servers, so problems with low disk space can be avoided.

Microsoft offers two free server virtualization solutions for Windows Server 2003 and Server 2008. Microsoft Virtual Server 2005 R2 SP2 is offered as a free download from Microsoft's Web site that provides support for guest and host operating systems running Windows Vista SP1 (Business, Enterprise, and Ultimate), Windows XP SP3 and Windows

Server 2008 (Standard, Enterprise, Datacenter, and Web). The software provides centralized management and administration of virtual servers, allowing for quick deployment of virtual servers that are reliable, secure and scalable. For host systems running Windows Server 2008, Microsoft has included the Hyper-V virtualization system with the Server 2008 operating system. Like the former, Hyper-V enables the consolidating of multiple server roles as separate virtual servers running on a single host system, allowing for different operating systems such as Linux, Windows, and others to run in parallel. Hyper-V was designed with enhanced security features in mind, providing an architecture that is less vulnerable to attack. This software includes a set of management and administration tools that can be used to both manage the host and virtual system's hardware from the same interface. Depending on the operating system of the host system, these are the two best software options for server virtualization, and because they are Microsoft products, they are fully supported.

Software licensing will also play a role in determining the ability to move to a virtualization environment. When using Microsoft Server 2003/2008 Enterprise Edition, licensing allows up to four virtual instances of the software on the same hardware system. This is one of the reasons the cost to purchase a single license of Enterprise Edition is much higher when compared to Standard Edition. For every other operating system, both server and desktop, an additional license will need to be purchased for each virtual server or machine desired. However, we strongly recommend that if you plan to implement a virtualization environment, the host system should run Microsoft Server 2008 Enterprise Edition, as Windows Server 2003 Enterprise Edition is no longer available from Microsoft.

Implementing a virtualization environment for your network will cost significantly less than purchasing multiple servers to individually accommodate your applications and services.

Peer-to-Peer

Many small firms use the built-in peer-to-peer network capabilities of their computer systems as an alternative to purchasing a server. A peer-to-peer network, in its simplest form, is two or more computers that can communicate with one another to share files and folders, printers, and applications, without using a server to accomplish these tasks. Peer-to-peer networks are commonly used in solo or small firm offices with only two or three computers. The computers, located on the same local network and belonging to the same Workgroup, can access shared resources in the Workgroups to which they are joined. A Workgroup is Microsoft's name for a peer-to-peer network. Unless a computer is joined to a Domain, it belongs to a Workgroup. By default, in Windows XP computers, the Workgroup name is "MSHOME," and in older versions of Windows the default Workgroup is called "WORKGROUP."

Peer-to-peer networks may sound like a good solution for small firms that have only a few computers, but there are some significant disadvantages when choosing to set up this type of network when compared to purchasing a server. First, when networking computers together, you are going to experience a slowdown and inconsistency in your system's performance. Workstations are not designed to handle concurrent accessing of their files by other computers. When this occurs, the system's resources are severely taxed, causing disruption to the users. Think of this as a tug of war for data. Your computer is trying to use data at the same time someone else needs it. Because of the inconsistency and unreliability of the peer-to-peer network, corruption of shared files such as case management and billing systems occurs frequently. Since computers in a peer-to-peer network can be running different operating systems, software incompatibilities between the systems can occur. The decentralization of critical firm data can lead to needlessly complex data backup scenarios, often resulting in important data not being backed up and protected. On top of all the issues above, the need to manage and administer multiple copies of the same software, such as anti-virus protection, on each individual computer becomes tiresome. Software that is centrally managed is much more cost-effective to purchase and maintain, as opposed to managing each computer's software suites independently.

There is an inaccurate perception that peer-to-peer networks save money and cost less than client/server networks. Yes, purchasing a server might seem expensive at first, even with lower-end units. However, in the end this is never the case. The costs of managing and maintaining a peer-to-peer network will always be higher than the costs that would have been incurred if you implemented a server/client network in the first place. Peer-to-peer networks can have higher licensing costs for software, because you are purchasing single licenses at a time. Software that is administered and maintained on independent computers will take more time to complete than if the software was centrally managed from a server. Technical support and consulting costs will be much higher in a peer-to-peer environment, and these are usually not considered when making the initial decision to use a peer-to-peer network. For most small network environments, even with those involving as few as two computers, purchasing a server to centralize applications and data can save time and money in the long run.

Server Operating Systems

Choosing a server's hardware components is just one step in selecting the right server. The second step is determining which operating system and software will be necessary to best meet both the current and future needs of the firm. There are many variations of server operating systems currently available, and they are described in detail below.

Microsoft Windows Server 2003 Standard Edition

The Windows Server 2003 server operating system was produced by Microsoft as the successor to Windows Server 2000 operating systems. The Windows Server 2003 server operating system delivers better performance, is more scalable, and offers more enhanced security than its predecessor. Microsoft Windows 2003 Server Standard Edition was released to target small to medium-sized businesses. The Standard Edition supports file and printer sharing, centralized desktop application deployment and enhanced security and access management through upgrades to Active Directory. Microsoft Windows 2003 Server Standard Edition supports up to four processors and 4 GB of memory.

Microsoft Windows Small Business Server 2003 Standard and Premium Editions

Microsoft SBS 2003 was developed and designed to offer small businesses an operating system that would provide a complete technology solution. The technologies integrated within Microsoft SBS include remote access, Remote Web Workplace, Terminal Services, enhanced security features, Fax Server, unified messaging console and enhanced monitoring and logging. The Standard Edition of SBS includes Windows SharePoint Services used for work collaboration, Microsoft Exchange Server 2003 for e-mail, Active Directory, and other features. The Premium Edition of Microsoft SBS 2003 includes Microsoft SQL Server 2000, Microsoft Internet Security and Acceleration Server 2004, and also everything included with SBS 2003 Standard Edition.

SBS Client Access Licenses (CALs) are more expensive than those for other editions of Windows. The reason for the cost increase is because the license for bundled software—e.g., Microsoft Exchange and Microsoft SQL Server—is included and is less expensive than buying licenses for all of the different products individually. The CALs can be purchased either for "per device" or "per user."

The SBS operating system bundle provides small businesses with a cost-effective complete solution, but does have some disadvantages or limitations:

(1) Only one computer in a domain can be running Windows SBS 2003

(2) Windows SBS 2003 is limited to 75 CALs (user or device)

(3) Windows SBS 2003 cannot be set up to trust any other domains

(4) Windows SBS 2003 is limited to a maximum of 4 GB of memory

(5) Terminal Services can operate only in Remote Administration mode for a maximum of two concurrent connections at once

Microsoft Windows Server 2003 Enterprise Edition

Microsoft Windows Server 2003 Enterprise Edition is aimed toward medium- to large-sized businesses that need a server capable of providing enterprise-level features and service. Such cases would be when a client runs applications that require more than 4 GB for smooth operation.

Microsoft Server 2003 Enterprise Edition supports up to eight processors and up to 32 GB of memory. Remember, Microsoft Windows Server 2003 Standard Edition and SBS support only up to four processors and 4 GB of memory. The Enterprise operating system also provides enterprise-class features such as clustering using Microsoft Cluster Server (MSCS). This operating system is recommended for servers that will be hosting database applications, case management applications or other software that requires large amounts of processing power and memory addressing—more than the Standard and SBS operating systems can support.

Microsoft Windows Server 2008

Microsoft Windows Server 2008 is the successor to Windows Server 2003 and was officially launched in late February 2008 and built from the same code base as Windows Vista. This does sound a bit scary after all of the problems we've experienced with Windows Vista, but hopefully Redmond got it right this time!

This operating system includes a lot of new features and enhancements such as native support for IPv6, new security features such as BitLocker and an improved Windows Firewall with a secure default configuration. Also, the manner in which this operating system handles processors and memory is different than previous versions. Processors and memory are now treated as plug and play devices, meaning they are "hot swappable." They can now be removed and replaced without shutting down the server.

Windows Server 2008 includes expanded Active Directory functionality, and a major upgrade to Terminal Services. Terminal Services now supports Remote Desktop Protocol 6.0, which provides the ability to share a single application over a Remote Desktop connection, rather than the entire Desktop, as had been the case before.

In previous versions of the Windows operating system, if corruption or errors were found on an NTFS volume, the volume would have to be dismounted and taken offline to correct errors. Windows Server 2008 supports a "self-healing" NTFS file system format that can detect and fix errors while online, without having to bring down the entire system. Microsoft Windows Server 2008 is offered in both 32- and 64-bit versions.

Windows Server 2008, like previous versions, is offered in the following editions:

- —Standard Edition
- —Enterprise Edition
- —Datacenter Edition
- —HPC Server
- —Web Server
- —Storage Server
- —Small Business Server
- —Essential Business Server

Most of the editions listed above would not be considered when purchasing a server solution for a small business or law firm and will not be discussed in this book. However, the Standard, Enterprise, and Small Business Server Editions are described below.

Microsoft Windows Small Business Server 2008 Standard and Premium Editions

Windows Small Business Server 2008 is based on Windows Server 2008 and includes Microsoft Exchange Server 2007 Standard Edition, Windows SharePoint Services 3.0, and trial subscriptions for Microsoft's new security products such as Forefront Security for Exchange.

The Small Business Server 2008 operating system was officially launched on November 12, 2008. Like previous editions of Small Business Server, the 2008 version is offered in both Standard and Premium Editions. The Standard Edition is regarded as a single server solution for small businesses—your "all-in-one" operating system. In one server, you get file and printer sharing, e-mail and Web hosting, and the ability to set up a domain for up to 75 users and/or devices. The Premium Edition contains all of the features and software that Standard Edition has, plus a license for Microsoft SQL Server 2008 Standard Edition. The Premium Edition requires two separate servers, one for Windows Server 2008 with Exchange, and the other solely for SQL Server. This is going to be a problem for small firms on a tight budget.

Windows SBS 2008 is offered only in a 64-bit version due to the requirements of Microsoft Exchange Server 2007, whose production version is 64-bit. This is an important distinction when considering your hardware purchase. Make sure you have 64-bit hardware if you are considering using these new modern server operating systems.

On a more positive note, Microsoft has finally changed the way CALs are purchased for SBS. In earlier editions, CALs could only be purchased in groups of 5/10/20 licenses, but not anymore. CALs for SBS 2008 can now be purchased individually. About time, Redmond!

Windows Server 2008 Standard Edition

Windows Server 2008 Standard Edition was designed to increase the reliability of your server infrastructure, while also saving time and reducing costs associated with server maintenance.

Standard Edition comes with enhanced security features to help protect your data and network, and includes powerful tools that give you greater control over your network. Windows Server 2008 Standard Edition comes with IIS 7.0, a powerful Web hosting and services platform. The operating system also includes Windows Server Hyper-V, virtualization software designed to support machine virtualization, along with an upgraded version of Terminal Services that supports Remote Desktop Protocol 6.0.

In terms of security, Standard Edition includes tools to improve auditing, secure startup and disk encryption using BitLocker. Standard Edition supports up to 32 GB of memory, four multi-core processors, and up to 250 concurrent Terminal Service connections.

Windows Server 2008 Enterprise Edition

Microsoft Windows Server 2008 Enterprise Edition, like its predecessor, is an operating system aimed at medium- to large-sized businesses looking for a server capable of handling enterprise-level services. Microsoft Server 2008 Enterprise Edition provides high availability of mission-critical applications through such features as failover clustering, fault-tolerant memory synchronization, and cross-file replication. This edition also features the latest advancements in security and is extremely scalable to support mission-critical applications.

This operating system is recommended for servers that will be hosting database applications, case management applications or other software that require large amounts of processing power and memory addressing, more than the Standard and SBS operating systems can support.

X64 Operating Systems

Thirty-two-bit processors have forever dominated the commercial marketplace, and, until recently, 64-bit processors were found only in supercomputers or very high-end and expensive servers. Now, however, 64-bit processors are more frequently offered as an option when configuring a server or a desktop computer to purchase. The 64-bit operating systems have been developed to run on these processors and offer some advantages over their 32-bit counterparts.

First, these systems process more data per clock cycle, and, second, they offer direct access to more virtual and physical memory than 32-bit systems. These advantages provide for more scalable, higher performing computing solutions. There are frequently device driver issues with X64 operating systems, however, so it's important to make sure everything is compatible before selecting these higher-end server operating systems.

Microsoft Windows 2003/2008 Standard Edition and Enterprise Edition operating systems are also offered in 64-bit versions, as well as Windows Small Business Server 2008.

MAC OS X Server "Leopard"

The Mac OS X Server 10.5 release code named "Leopard" was released for Mac servers on October 26, 2007. OS X version 10.5 includes applications to allow administrators to more easily manage their users and computers, host Web sites, and e-mail and to provide services such as file and printer sharing. Mac OS X Server combines proprietary Apple applications and open-source technologies to provide administrators with a powerful toolset that rivals the features and functionality provided by Windows-based operating systems. Mac OS X Server allows for groups of employees to collaborate and communicate through an internal Wiki Web site that comes complete with calendar, blog and mailing list functionality. Users can create and edit their own Wiki pages, tag, upload files, and materials, and search.

Mac OS X Server "Snow Leopard"

Mac OS X Server 10.6 is the upcoming version of the Mac OS X server operating system, and will include new features and software such as iCal Server 2, Podcast Producer 2, and new Address Book server capabilities. Snow Leopard operating system uses a 64-bit kernel, allowing for the support of greater amounts of memory and number of multicore processors. The release date for this operating system has not been set, but speculation is that it will be available by the third quarter of 2009.

Linux-Based Operating Systems

Linux-based operating systems are similar to Unix-based operating systems and are built on an open-source kernel packaged with system utilities, software, and libraries. The underlying source code of the operating system can be freely modified, used, and redistributed.

Linux is now packaged for different uses, primarily servers, which contain modified kernels along with a variety of software packages tailored to different requirements. Some of the commercially available distributions that are backed by corporations are Fedora (Red Hat), SUSE Linux (Novell), Ubuntu (Canoical Ltd), and Mandriva Linux. Each of these distributions has versions specifically designed and programmed to run on server-based hardware to provide management, Web and e-mail hosting services, file and printer sharing, along with other services and functionality that are available in both Mac and Windows-based server operating systems.

CHAPTER SEVEN

Networking Hardware

NETWORKING HARDWARE TYPICALLY REFERS to equipment that allows network devices to communicate with one another, but not always. Some other types of networking hardware can include server racks, cabling, and other devices that help make up the computer network. Below, we provide descriptions and recommendations for the most common types of networking hardware.

Switches

A switch is a piece of networking hardware that connects network segments (discrete sections of the network). For example, if two computers are connected into the same switch and are located within the same IP network, the switch will allow these two devices to communicate. Switches inspect data packets as they are received and, based on the source and destination addresses, will forward the packet appropriately. By delivering the packet of information only to the device it was intended for, network bandwidth is preserved and the information is delivered in a much quicker manner. As a comparison, hubs send the traffic to all ports, irrespective of the destination device. Switches have all but replaced network hubs, which you rarely will see in a production environment anymore. Unlike hubs, switches are "intelligent" devices and can operate on more than one layer of the Open Systems Interconnection (OSI) model, such as a multi-layer switch. Switches allow traffic to pass through them at speeds of 10 Mbps, 100 Mbps, 1 Gbps, or 10 Gbps, depending on the speeds of the ports.

Most solo and small law firms will not need expensive, high-end network switches for their computer infrastructure. In the majority of situations, a switch is needed only to connect computer workstations to the server and the Internet and nothing more. NETGEAR offers reasonably priced switches in a variety of configurations to meet almost any solo or small firm need. The ProSafe Unmanaged Desktop series is a good choice for the solo or small law firm, because of the low cost, ease of set-up, and reliability.

When purchasing a switch for your business, you will need to determine the amount of connections or ports the switch will serve. Next, you will have to determine the speeds of the ports that you will require. Will all of your computers need to connect to the server at Gigabyte speeds, or just a handful of devices? Remember, you certainly will pay more for a 48-port switch with 48-GB ports than if you bought a 48-port switch with only 2-GB ports. The ProSafe Unmanaged Desktop Switches from NETGEAR can be found on their Web site at **www.netgear.com**.

NETGEAR
ProSafe Unmanaged
Desktop Switch

Entry-level and Intermediate-level Routers

A router is a computer-networking device that connects networks together, e.g., your business local network to your Internet provider's network. A router's job is to determine the proper path for data to travel between the networks and to forward data packets to the next device along the path. Routers come in all shapes and sizes and with different features. For a solo or small firm, a basic router will be sufficient to connect the local network to the Internet, as well as protect computers and other hardware devices on the local network from outside attacks. A basic router will require little configuration from the default values to get it configured and communicating with the Internet Provider's network. Most basic routers are only capable of handling broadband Internet connections such as cable or DSL. If your firm has a T-1 or any variant of this Internet connection, you will most likely be provided with a router by your Internet provider.

A router well-suited for the solo or small firm is the Linksys EtherFast Cable/DSL Router with four-port switch. This router will allow you to share your high-speed cable or DSL Internet connection with multiple computers, and the built-in four-port switch allows you to daisy-chain additional switches to the router as you add more devices to your network.

The Linksys EtherFast router supports Dynamic Host Control Protocol (DHCP), Universal Plug-and-Play (UpnP), Demilitarized Zone (DMZ) and Network Address Translation (NAT). The Linksys EtherFast router can act as a DHCP server, providing Internet Protocol addresses to all of the computers on the network, enabling the clients to quickly access the Internet with minimal configuration. The Linksys EtherFast router has some built-in firewall capabilities and allows for advanced security management function for port-filtering/forwarding, MAC address filtering and DMZ hosting.

The router supports IPSec and PPTP Pass-through, which is important if your firm supports remote access through a Virtual Private Network (VPN) connection, which is an encrypted secure communication channel. The router can be administered and upgraded through the local Web interface, as well as remotely if remote administration is enabled and configured. The included set-up wizard walks you through the configuration of the device with step-by-step instructions as well as connecting it to the Internet. The Linksys EtherFast Cable/DSL Router is also available in an eight-port switch model. The Linksys EtherFast Cable/DSL Router with four-port switch can be purchased from your local electronics or computer store for approximately $50 or online at **www.linksys.com**.

Linksys EtherFast Cable/DSL Router with 4-Port Switch

If your firm needs an upgraded firewall with additional features and greater flexibility than the Linksys EtherFast provides, an alternative solution is the Juniper product line. The Juniper Networks Secure Services Gateway 5 (SSG5) or SSG20 are two security appliances that provide great performance, enhanced security and management for small office deployments. The SSG devices offer Unified Threat Management (UTM) security that scans incoming and outgoing traffic for viruses, spyware, spam, and other malicious threats. The UTM security feature allows flexibility for the device to be deployed as a stand-alone security device or in coordination with other anti-spyware, anti-virus and anti-spam solutions. These firewall security devices are well worth the cost, and if looking for an upgrade, offer the perfect routing solution. The Juniper SSG devices start at around $550 and can be purchased online. The price will vary depending on the accompanying modules, if any, that you purchase with the

device. We also strongly recommend that you
purchase support for the device, which will
include firmware updates and technical support if needed.

Juniper Networks SSG5 Router

Firewalls/IDS Devices

An intrusion detection system (IDS) is used to identify many types of
malicious network traffic and computer usage that can't be recognized by
a conventional firewall. These attacks include network attacks against vulnerable services (Web hosting, e-mail), data-driven attacks on applications, host-based attacks such as privilege escalation, unauthorized
logins, and access to sensitive files. Privilege escalation is the act of
exploiting a vulnerability in an application to gain access to resources
that would have otherwise been protected from being accessed. IDSs also
can detect and prevent malware such as viruses, Trojan horses, and worms
from entering the network.

An IDS device is commonly placed at the computer network's gateway so
that all incoming and outgoing network traffic must pass through the
device. This allows the device to scan all incoming traffic before it is
passed on to the local computer network. A firewall can permit or deny
data traffic based on port number, originating or receiving Internet protocol (IP) address and protocol type, just to name a few capabilities. An IP
address is a unique address assigned to a networked device, such as a computer that allows the device to communicate with other networked
devices. Just think of an IP address as being the same as a home address,
which is a unique way to identify your home's physical location.

A firewall device is important to the protection and security of any computer equipment that has an Internet connection. For those users that
have a broadband Internet connection at home, a firewall should also be
used to protect your home systems and networks from outside attacks.
This is especially important for those attorneys who work from home,
because you do not want your client's data to become compromised.

The Cisco ASA 5500 Series Adaptive-Security Appliances offer a good solution for solo and small firms looking to protect their local business network from outside attacks. This appliance integrates a world-class firewall,
unified communications (voice/video) security, SSL (Secure Socket Layer)
and IPSec (Internet protocol security) VPN, intrusion prevention and con-

tent security services into a single piece of hardware. Combining all of the functionality into one piece of network hardware eliminates the need to purchase a single device for each function. This saves time in both set-up and configuration, eliminates complexity, and tremendously reduces the cost to secure your business computer network.

The Cisco ASA 5500 Series provides intelligent threat defense and secure communications services that stop attacks before they can impact your firm's business continuity. The firewall technology is built upon the proven capabilities of the Cisco PIX family of security appliances, allowing valid traffic to flow in and out of the local network while keeping out unwelcome visitors. The URL and content filtering technologies implemented by the device protect the business as well as the employees from the theft of confidential and proprietary information, as well as help the business comply with Federal regulations such as HIPAA and Gramm-Leach-Bliley. The application control capabilities can limit peer-to-peer and instant messaging traffic, which often lead to security vulnerabilities and the introduction of viruses and threats to the network. The implementation of a Cisco ASA 5000 Series device will deliver comprehensive multilayer security to your computer network and will help you to sleep better at night knowing your electronic data and equipment are protected. The Cisco ASA 5500 Series Adaptive-Security Appliance can be purchased from Cisco Systems online at **www.cisco.com**.

The cost of the Cisco ASA 5500 Series device will range in the thousands of dollars, depending on the number of licenses, warranty, and support purchased with the product. When purchasing this device, we absolutely recommend getting SmartNet maintenance. SmartNet allows you access to the excellent technical support personnel of Cisco, hardware replacement for failures, and upgrades to the device operating system. Make no mistake about it—this is an excellent high-end firewall well worth the investment to protect your network and client data.

Cisco ASA 5500 Series
Adaptive Security
Appliance Devices

Racks

A rack unit or enclosure is a piece of hardware that is used to store, organize, and secure your equipment. Most often, rack units are used to hold rack mount servers. There are many types of computer and networking hardware that are offered in rack mount sizes. This is because of the desire to locate and secure equipment in a single location. Rack units can be portable (for example, mounted on caster wheels), bolted into the floor, or mounted on the wall if small enough. Depending on the amount of space that is available for the servers and networking equipment, this information will greatly affect which type of rack to purchase. The leading manufacturers of rack units and enclosures are American Power Conversion (APC) and Chatsworth.

APC NetShelter SX enclosures are rack enclosures with advanced cooling, power distribution, and cable management for server and networking devices. The 19-inch rack is vendor neutral and is guaranteed to be compatible with all EIA-310 compliant 19-inch equipment, which nearly all "rack-mountable" equipment is. The enclosures offer large cable access slots in the roof to provide overhead cable egress. This is great when cables come down through the ceiling. The bottom design allows for unobstructed cable access through a raised floor. The enclosures have perforated front and rear doors to provide ample ventilation for servers and other networking hardware that require unobstructed air flow. The front and rear doors can be rearranged so that they can swing open in either direction, depending on the room's layout.

The enclosure contains rear cable management channels to assist in managing the plethora of cables the servers and network equipment require. The frame design of the NetShelter SX Enclosures is made with heavy-gauge mounting rails and casters to provide support for up to 3,000 lbs of equipment. APC's NetShelter SX enclosures are offered in four different

APC NetShelter
SX Enclosures

sizes and can be purchased with accessories such as UPS (Uninterruptible Power Supply) battery back-ups, retractable keyboard and mouse pad, flip-down monitor, cable management arms, additional fans, and power distribution centers. The APC NetShelter SX rack enclosures can be purchased online at their Web site (**www.apc.com**), and the basic enclosures start at around $1,500.

Cabling

Now that you have all of your equipment selected and purchased, you will need to decide how to wire your data network and what network patch cables should be purchased to connect your computers to the network drops (cables from the wall outlet to the hub/switch location). These patch cables come in various lengths and are primarily offered in two different types. First, you have the category 5e cable, which is not the same as the generically termed Cat5 specification. Second, you have the category 6 cable, more commonly referred to as "cat6."

The cat6 standard cable is starting to gain popularity as more and more networking and computer devices operate and communicate at Gigabit speeds. Current data transfer rates and applications operating at one Gigabyte per second speeds are starting to push the limits of category 5 cabling, although category 5e cable is rated for Gigabit speeds. The trends of the past and predictions for the future indicate that data rates have been doubling every 18 months. The category 6 cables offer double the amount of bandwidth capacity over category 5 cables, and a better transmission performance. The category 6 cable provides a higher signal-to-noise ratio, allowing for higher reliability for current applications and higher data rates for the future. Analysts have indicated that nearly 80 to 90 percent of all new wiring installations are using cat6 cabling. This would lead to a fairly easy purchasing decision, because all cat6 cabling is backward-compatible with cat 5 cabling, and allows for straightforward replacement of cat5 cables.

There hasn't been any movement or enhancement to cable specifications since our last edition. Cable technology has actually remained flat for more than 12 months. If your firm is planning on wiring the office for data and voice, from a future perspective, it makes all the sense in the world to have your office wired with cat6 cabling. Remember, once the dust has settled from the construction, it would be extremely costly to have any type of cabling pulled out and replaced. The 20 percent premium that you currently will pay for cat6 cabling over cat5 cabling is worth the added cost.

Wireless Networking Devices

A wireless networking device allows for the communication between devices without being physically connected by wires. In a solo or small firm, if the investment cost to wire an office space with data cables is too expensive, a wireless solution may be the answer. This is particularly true in older properties—and may be aesthetically desirable in historic premises. A wireless network is extremely convenient for attorneys who use laptops as their primary computers because they can move from their office to the conference room with their laptop and still stay connected to the local network and Internet. The cost to purchase a wireless networking device is extremely low and the benefits gained are worth the investment. However, do not implement a wireless network without taking the proper security precautions. By default, most wireless routers and access points are preconfigured not to enable encryption on wireless connections. This means that, by default, all communications between computers and the wireless device are unencrypted and are not secure. How many people have connected their laptop to an unencrypted wireless network so that they could check their e-mail or perform online banking? We see this all the time—even at legal technology conferences!

Wireless networks should be set up with the proper security. First and foremost, encryption should be enabled on the wireless device. Whether using Wired Equivalent Privacy (WEP) 128-bit or WPA encryption, make sure that all communications are secure. WEP is a weaker layer and can be cracked if sufficient data is captured, though the reality is that hackers will go for unsecured networks before going after any secured network. Frankly, the Federal Trade Commission and the Canadian Privacy Comisioner have both found WEP insufficient to secure credit card information, so we suggest it not be used at all. Second, if the wireless network is for the firm only, enable MAC (Media Access Control) filtering on the wireless device. MAC filtering essentially limits the devices that may communicate with the wireless device. If the MAC address of a computer's wireless network card does not match an authorized MAC address, then the wireless device will not communicate with the unauthorized computer. This is an added layer of security. Most commonly, wireless routers and access points ship with default network names such as "LINKSYS" or "NETGEAR." While in operation, these devices will broadcast their names so that wireless clients can locate the wireless networks. It is strongly recommended, for security reasons, that the default name of the wireless network be changed and that SSID (Service Set Identifier, which is essentially the network name) broadcasting be disabled.

Linksys is a popular manufacturer of wireless networking devices for home and small to medium-sized businesses. The Linksys Wireless-G Broadband Router is an all-in-one Internet sharing router with a four-port switch. Like the wired router discussed earlier, this router can be used to connect your computer network to the Internet, with the added functionality of a wireless network. The 802.11g wireless standard protocol is used by this device and offers data transmission speeds up to 54 Mbps. This standard is about five times as fast as the 802.11b standard, which offered data transmission speeds up to 11 Mbps. One of the benefits of the 802.11g standard is that it is backward-compatible with 802.11b devices.

Recently, there has been a push by wireless device manufacturers to get consumers to purchase their 802.11n wireless products. The proposed 802.11n standard is still only in draft form and has not been approved. It has been a couple of years now and nobody is willing to predict when the 802.11n standard will be approved, if at all. We do not recommend purchasing an 802.11n-compatible product at this point because it is not certain what specification the final form will take. If you do ignore our advice and purchase 802.11n products, make sure that everything is from the same manufacturer, a strategy that will give you a greater chance of connection success.

The Linksys Wireless-G Broadband Router comes with advanced security features such as Wi-Fi Protected Access (WPA) and WEP encryption, wireless MAC filtering, powerful SPI (Stateful Packet Inspection) firewall, and other security features. SPI allows the firewall to track each data connection traversing across the interfaces of the device to make sure that each packet of information is valid and not harmful. The Linksys Wireless-G Broadband Router can be purchased from your local electronics or computer store for around $70, or online from the Linksys Web site at **www.linksys.com**.

Linksys Wireless-G Broadband Router

CHAPTER EIGHT

Miscellaneous Hardware

ASIDE FROM ALL OF the computer hardware, software, and networking equipment, there are other pieces of hardware that deserve to be discussed, whether they provide mobility, security, or functionality that would benefit a solo or small firm.

Fire safe

A fire safe is an important piece of hardware to have in your office to protect your backup tapes, software licenses, and other valuables from destruction during a fire. You don't want to lose your only set of backup tapes or backup hard drive in a fire!

It is strongly recommended that you store backup tapes, software licenses, copies of technical contracts with third parties and other important documents in a fire safe. Purchasing one is a relatively inexpensive investment—perhaps a couple of hundred dollars through your local office supply store. There are many sizes and shapes of fire safes, so you shouldn't have a problem finding one that suits your needs. The key specification is the rated internal temperature. The safe may be rated to keep the contents from burning, but it also should not damage the contents (for example, by melting of the tape casing), which is why the internal rated temperature is important.

Also, always make sure the fire safe is kept closed; what good would an open fire safe do in the event of a fire? We can't count the number of clients who cannot resist the convenience of keeping the fire safe open.

If you are going to buy a fire safe, give it a chance to afford the protection it offers.

Battery Backup Devices

A battery backup device is an electronic device that supplies secondary power in the absence of main power, such as during a power outage. The battery backup will supply power when it detects an outage. Battery backup devices can also protect electronic hardware from power spikes, dirty electricity, and power outages. They make battery backup devices in all sizes and power capacities, and depending on what devices you are looking to protect, this will affect the size and capacities you choose. APC is the leading manufacturer of battery backup devices used for protecting computers, servers, and other networking hardware.

It is strongly recommended that every computer within the local network be placed on a battery backup device, such as the APC Back-UPS CS 350. At our office, we have all of our computers, printers, routers, switches, phone, and voicemail system on battery backup devices to protect our hardware investment. This device will supply your computer with power for up to five minutes after an outage has occurred. During this interval, the battery backup device will communicate with the APC software that came bundled with the device and will allow the computer to shut down properly.

Many computers will experience software or hardware errors after a power outage because they did not have the opportunity to shut down

APC Back-UPS CS 350

properly. When computers and (horror of horrors) servers go down hard, the result is often not pretty. There is a great chance for data loss or system failure in the event of an outage. By purchasing battery backup devices for your computers and other electronic equipment, you are protecting your hardware and software investment and avoiding possible IT costs to correct all the problems that might ensue from a hard power down. The APC Back-UPS CS 350 can be purchased from APC's Web site (**www.apc.com**) for $69.99.

That takes care of battery backup devices for computers, but what about servers? Servers require more power to operate than a desktop or laptop computer. Therefore, they will require more power to allow them to operate during a power outage. On top of that, they take much longer to shut down properly than a workstation, due to the greater number of services and processes constantly running on a server. The average server will take upwards of 15 minutes or more to properly shut down, so supplying this server with enough power to accomplish this task is important. Certainly, you do not want your server to experience a "hard" shutdown because the risk is still great for data loss or hardware failure.

Battery backup devices for servers can be purchased as a tower unit or rack mountable, depending on what your firm needs to support its server configuration.

The APC Smart-UPS 1500VA is an ideal battery backup solution to protect a server from power outages, power spikes or dirty electricity that can damage the server's internal hardware components. The Smart-UPS 1500VA is offered in both tower and rack-mountable forms and can supply the server with enough power to allow the server to shut down properly. Note that this unit only has enough capacity to supply power to one server and its peripheral devices. If there is a need to purchase a battery backup device for multiple servers, there are models with greater capacities that will be able to handle the load.

As with all batteries, they will need to be replaced eventually. Happily, the batteries in these devices are hot-swappable, which means they can be replaced without the need to shut down the battery backup device or the devices connected to the unit. It is important to replace batteries as soon as they fail so that the systems connected to the battery backup devices continue to be protected during power failures. Replacement batteries for these devices can be purchased online from APC's Web site. Because the batteries in these units are replaceable, this is one hardware investment that you will not be replacing every one to two years. In our experience, these devices usually will outlast the life of the computers connected to them.

The APC Smart-UPS 1500VA comes bundled with software that can be installed on the server itself to enable the battery backup device to communicate with the server. This is necessary so that, if a power outage occurs, the battery backup can alert the server to begin the shutdown process. The battery backup device is connected to the server through a USB or serial cable. The APC Smart-UPS 1500VA can be purchased from APC's Web site for $559.

APC Smart-UPS Models

Fax Machines

Even though the need for fax machines has dwindled, they are still a staple in a law office. Sometimes, there just isn't enough time to scan a document and then e-mail it to a recipient, and instead the document will be faxed. We still see plenty of solos and small firms where there is no interest in learning how to scan. The fax machine is the devil they know, and they don't want to change. So even with all of the advancements with technology, the fax machine has a continued role. As previously stated, many digital copiers have fax transmission/receipt capabilities. Check with your vendor representative to see if using the copier is more cost-effective.

The Brother IntelliFax-2920 is a high-speed laser fax, phone, and copier. This model was designed for the small business, in which multiple users can easily share the benefits of this fully featured laser fax machine. Its design incorporates a high capacity, front-loading paper tray (which can adjust to hold letter or legal size paper) that makes replenishing the paper an easy task that doesn't require a degree in engineering to accomplish.

The IntelliFax-2920 is equipped with 16 MB of memory, allowing multiple faxes to be stored in memory for transmission when the line is free. The 33.6 Kbps SuperG3 fax modem optimizes throughput transmitting as fast as two seconds per page. The front-loading paper tray has a 250-sheet paper capacity that is easily accessible and reduces time spent reloading paper. The paper tray can adjust to hold either letter or legal size paper. Access to incoming faxes can be protected through the use of a password, assuring that only the appropriate parties see the confidential faxes.

Finally, if your needs exceed or grow beyond just faxing and copying, this device comes with an USB interface and can serve as a laser printer capable of printing up to 15 pages per minute. This device comes with a standard one-year limited warranty. The Brother IntelliFax-2920 can be purchased online at Brother's Web site (**www.brother-usa.com**) for around $300.

Brother IntelliFax-2920

Backup Solutions

As hard drive sizes get larger and the volume of electronic data created increases, larger media is required to store the daily, weekly and monthly backup files. Luckily, the days of having to purchase expensive tape drives, autoloaders, and media has long passed. The options for media to store backups have increased and the cost for many of these viable options has decreased at the same time. Solo and small firms do not need to purchase or implement an expensive backup system. In general, a set of inexpensive external hard drives will do the trick. They offer more capacity than most tape media, are portable, and are relatively inexpensive. And don't forget that you should keep at least one complete backup set off-site in the event that your entire office is lost—or inaccessible—during a disaster.

Depending on the backup system that has been implemented, a lot of storage space may be needed, especially if your firm has implemented a system where a full backup job is run on a nightly basis. The Iomega UltraMax Pro Desktop Hard Drive adds secure, high capacity storage to your computer system. The triple interface (FireWire 800, 400 and USB 2.0) allows the hard drive to deliver transfer rates up to 800 Mbps and can be connected to any computer or server that has these types of connections.

The high-performance drive comes preconfigured in a RAID-0 hard disk configuration for higher data throughput, but also can be configured in a RAID-1 hard disk configuration if you prefer. The RAID-1 hard disk configuration provides better fault tolerance but you loose half of the storage space for disk mirroring. Nevertheless, we recommend using a RAID-1 hard disk configuration when configuring the device to store your backup files.

The Iomega UltraMax Pro Desktop Hard Drive has a storage capacity of 1.5 TB, made up of two 750 GB SATA hard drives. The hard drives are hot swappable allowing for business continuity and easy replacement. The unit also comes with a power adapter and connection cables to connect the device to a computer or server. If you have not yet purchased backup software, the device comes bundled with EMC Retrospect Express backup software that can be installed and used on both a computer and server to backup your system and data files. The device comes with a standard 1-year warranty. The Iomega ULtraMax Pro Desktop Hard Drive can be purchased online from Iomega's web site (**www.iomega.com**) for around $380.

Iomega UltraMax Pro Desktop Hard Drive

As an alternative to using a local backup solution, remote backup solutions are becoming more commonplace. Remote backup service providers backup your data over the Internet and store your data on their systems. This type of service eliminates the need for users to change backup tapes or external hard drives. Most backup service providers also have a piece of hardware that will sit on your local network, allowing for a quick recovery from a disaster, such as a server failure. While most of your data backups may be stored offsite, the piece of hardware on your local network may contain the most recent backup allowing your business to get up and running as soon as possible. This eliminates the need to wait for media to be shipped or your most recent backup files to be downloaded before recovery can begin.

There are a number of things to take into consideration when evaluating backup service providers. First, protection of your data and privacy is of the utmost importance. Make sure that all of your data is encrypted in both transmission and in storage. No exceptions. And make sure that you are the only one with the key or pass phrase to unlock your data.

Consider the time it will take to recover from a server failure. How long will it take to get your system back up and running? Be careful of the cost per gigabyte (GB) of storage. Don't underestimate the volume of data you will be backing up. Data will accumulate quickly and so will the cost for storage. Plan carefully. Finally, make sure that you own your data. Never allow any service provider to "own" your data as many will require large fees in order to return your data to you should you choose to take your business elsewhere.

Some of the remote backup solution providers to consider are Zenith (**www.zenithinfotech.com**), i365 (**www.evault.com**) and Iron Mountain (**www.ironmountain.com**). Each of these companies offer different services and charge varying rates, so do your homework before proceeding with a remote backup solution provider.

Smartphones

Smartphones have become the number one tech accessory among lawyers. It wasn't too long ago when a lawyer would carry two separate devices, a cell phone and a personal digital assistant (PDA). The cell phone was used to make phone calls and the PDA was used to keep your notes and calendar—some even allowed you to view your e-mail, captured during your last synchronization with your work computer. Since that time, everything has changed. Smartphones are becoming more and more like laptops, able to perform almost every function a laptop can, but at a tenth of the size, and, with so many capabilities, attorneys regard them as a necessity. That trend is moving downward to solos and small firms as well.

The smartphone debate has largely involved two major players, the Black-Berry and the Palm Treo, also known as the "BlackBerry Killer." The nick-name derives from the fact that no separate BlackBerry Enterprise server (BES) is required—the Palm Treos (those running Windows Mobile) use the Windows operating system. The BES is required to interface the mail system with the actual BlackBerry device. The Treo has built-in support to wirelessly synchronize with an Exchange server, thereby not requiring the cost of the server or BES licenses.

Some solos don't host their own e-mail and instead retrieve mail from their ISP. BlackBerry users in this type of configuration typically install a desktop application to their computer that synchronizes with their phone. This requires that the computer be left on and connected to the Internet, which is a security problem. The debate over which phone is better, more feature-rich, and compatible has been going on for some time and probably will continue to rage for years to come.

Recently, Apple released its newest version of the iPhone, replacing the first generation iPhones with a product that contains a greater amount of memory, increased features and functionality, and is more business friendly. Building on a strong consumer following from the first genera-tion iPhone, and looking to solidify its place in the smartphone market-place, Apple has added support for Microsoft Exchange e-mail by licens-ing ActiveSync from Microsoft. The new iPhone is now "enterprise-ready" and supports over-the-air synchronization of e-mail, calendar, and con-tacts with a Microsoft Exchange Server; however, the phone natively lacks support for rich document editing and creation, requiring users to pur-chase third-party software to complete these tasks.

The iPhone, however, doesn't appear ready to take over the corporate smartphone market just yet—in fact, it is more suited for your teenager than your business.

A chart below is provided that compares some of the features of the most popular smartphone models.

	RIM BlackBerry 8310 Curve	Palm Treo 750	Samsung BlackJack II	Apple iPhone 3G
Price	$199.99 w/ 2-Year Contract (AT&T)	$529.00 Unlocked, $349.99 w/ 2-Year Contract (AT&T)	$199.99 w/ 2-Year Contract (AT&T)	$199.99 w/2-Year Contract (8GB AT&T), $299.99 w/ 2-Year Contract (16GB AT&T)
Weight (oz)	3.9	5.4	3.5	4.7
Dimensions (inches)	4.2" x 2.3" x 0.6"	4.4" x 2.3" x 0.8"	4.4" x 2.3" x 0.4"	4.5" x 2.4" x 0.48"
Estimated Battery Life	Talk Time: 4 Hours	Talk Time: 4 Hours	Talk Time: 7 Hours	Talk Time: 8 Hours
Screen Size	2.5"	2.5"	2.4"	3.5"
Screen Resolution (Pixels)	320 x 240	240 x 240	320 x 240	480 x 320
Display Surface	Plastic	Plastic	Plastic	Glass
Built-in Memory	64MB	128MB	256MB	8GB/16GB
Camera	2 Megapixels	1.3 Megapixles	2 Megapixels	2 Megapixels
Data Network	3G, EDGE	3G	3G, EDGE	3G, EDGE, WiFi
Keyboard	Physical	Physical	Physical	Virtual
Operating System	BlackBerry	Windows Mobile	Windows Mobile	Mac OS X
Carrier Choice	AT&T	AT&T, Unlocked GSM	AT&T	AT&T

From reviewing the chart, you can get a sense as to what each of the model's capabilities are and/or what each of the devices may be lacking.

We strongly recommend the use of the Palm Treo 750 (700w/wx) or the newly released 800w. The Palm Treo 750 (700w/wx) is the current generation of the Palm Treo smartphones and offers some enhanced and great new features. The Palm Treo 750 (700w/wx) combines a GSM (global system for mobile communication) phone, e-mail messaging, and Web browsing into one easy-to-use, stylish device.

The Treo 750 (700w/wx) runs Microsoft Windows Mobile 6.1 software, supports Exchange ActiveSync, Microsoft Office and PDF documents, Bluetooth wireless, and other standard phone features such as text messaging, camera, and video recorder. Microsoft Exchange ActiveSync with Direct Push Technology lets you wirelessly synchronize your smartphone with your company's Exchange e-mail server to send and receive e-mail, update your calendar, contacts, tasks, and respond to meeting invitations. You can be on the road and still receive your e-mail on a current basis. Changes you make to your e-mail on the phone will be updated on the Microsoft Exchange Server over the air. E-mail, calendar, tasks—all can be sent and received wirelessly in "real time."

Enhanced security features include remote data wiping and device password enforcements—everything is synchronized using SSL (Secure Socket Layer). The remote data wipe feature can be enacted in the event that a phone is lost. An administrator can then remotely wipe the data from the phone using an interface directly built into Microsoft Exchange Server. This will help to protect private and confidential data if a phone is stolen or lost. The Palm Treo 750 (700w/wx) comes with Microsoft Office Word Mobile, Excel Mobile, PowerPoint Mobile, and Piscel PDF Viewer. These productivity solutions will allow you to open, review and modify documents while on the go.

The Palm Treo 800w was recently released and is only offered by Sprint. The Treo 800w is the first Sprint smartphone to ship with EV-DO Rev. A. support right out of the box, offering download speeds up to 1.4 Mbps, although this falls way short when compared to the surfing speeds of 3G compatible phones. The Treo 800w also comes with both WiFi and GPS support. The phone supports both 802.11b and 802.11g networks, and using the GPS radio, you can now get navigational directions right from your phone.

The Treo 800w also contains some minor upgrades from previous Treo models that include a higher resolution and bigger display screen, the Windows Mobile 6.1 operating system, and has 128 MB of program memory and 256 MB of user memory. The phone also includes all of the Windows Mobile staples such as Microsoft Mobile Office Suite, a PDF reader and support for Microsoft's Direct Push Technology for real-time e-mail delivery and synchronization with your Exchange server.

The Palm Treo 750 (700w/wx) and 800w can be purchased from Palm's Web site (**www.palm.com**) or from your local cellular service provider such as Sprint, Cingular Wireless, or Verizon Wireless.

These devices are not cheap and can run over $500; however, they are generally discounted by most carriers. Older versions of the Windows-based Treos carry similar features but may require more frequent rebooting as a result of being "memory-challenged." The newer models have more memory available for the phone operation and are more desirable. You may not be able to get the phone model you want if it is not supported by your cellular carrier.

The key message is that any Windows Mobile-based phone will provide immediate integration with your Exchange messaging server. We prefer the Treo line, but Samsung makes some great models, too. We recommend that you choose your wireless carrier first and then see what Windows Mobile-based phones it provides.

Over-the-air synchronization with Exchange Public folders is a requested feature by many solo and small firm lawyers. You may require a third party server implementation such as Goodlink to perform these functions. Another alternative may be to install special software on your computer to synchronize with the Public Folders. Your computer must be powered up and logged into Outlook for the over-the-air synchronization to occur. As you can imagine, this is a potential security vulnerability and must be carefully considered and engineered.

On a side note, everyone is familiar with getting spam in their in-boxes, but how about on your phone? Spam text messages can be costly, since most carriers will charge for both text messages sent and received. There is no anti-SMS-spam software available to install on cell phones to prevent the transmission of these messages, but there is nevertheless a simple way to stop it. The vast majority of spam text messages originate on the Internet, not from other cell phones. Why? Because the spammers don't have to pay anything when using the Internet to send the text messages. Most carriers, led by AT&T and Verizon Wireless, offer spam SMS blocking features. To enable this feature, just log into your online account managers and the options should be available within your account profile. Sprint and T-Mobile currently only allow you to block SMS messages from certain phone numbers and addresses. What are you waiting for? We've signed up.

AT&T (**mymessages.wireless.att.com**)

Verizon Wireless (**vtext.com**)

Sprint (**www.sprint.com**)

T-Mobile (**www.t-mobile.com**)

CHAPTER NINE

Productivity Software

HAVING WORKED WITH SO many solos and small law firms through the years, we know that attorneys are constantly striving to be more productive. As a result, we're always asked if we recommend that attorneys use Corel WordPerfect or Microsoft Word.

Well the short answer is Word. This is what the business world uses. There are alternatives, but they all come with some degree of pain. Many adherents for WordPerfect are religious in their fervor and others are evangelical in their admiration for open source solutions. Whether you're a fan of Microsoft or not, the reality is that Word is the preferred application of the business world and your clients will expect you to use it. They will not appreciate any conversion problems that occur if you are using something else. In this section we detail the latest and greatest releases of productivity software that can help your attorneys be more productive.

Microsoft Office

Microsoft Office 2007 is the most recent version of Microsoft's productivity suite. The retail release of this product coincided with the release of Microsoft Vista, back in late January 2007. Microsoft Office 2007 contains many new features, the most notable of which is the graphical user interface called Ribbon (except in Outlook 2007 it is called Explorer), which replaces the standard menus and toolbars we have all grown accustomed to over the years. Microsoft Office 2007 is offered in eight different versions, with each of the different version suites described in the chart on the next page.

	Microsoft Office Basic 2007	Microsoft Office Home & Student 2007	Microsoft Office Standard 2007	Microsoft Office Small Business 2007	Microsoft Office Professional 2007	Microsoft Office Ultimate 2007	Microsoft Office Professional Plus 2007	Microsoft Office Enterprise 2007
Microsoft Office Word 2007	●	●	●	●	●	●	●	●
Microsoft Office Excel 2007	●	●	●	●	●	●	●	●
Microsoft Office PowerPoint 2007		●	●	●	●	●	●	●
Microsoft Office Outlook 2007	●		●				●	●
Microsoft Office Outlook 2007 with Business Contact Manager				●	●	●		
Microsoft Office Accounting Express 2007				●	●	●		
Microsoft Office Publisher 2007				●	●	●	●	●
Microsoft Office Access 2007					●	●	●	●
Microsoft Office InfoPath 2007						●	●	●
Microsoft Office Groove 2007						●		●
Microsoft Office OneNote 2007		●				●		●
Microsoft Office Communicator 2007							●	●
Integrated Enterprise Content Management						●	●	●
Integrated Electronic Forms						●	●	●
Advanced Information Rights Management and Policy Capabilities						●	●	●

The majority of solo and small firms will require only the Small Business or Professional Editions.

Some of the new features that you will see in the latest edition of Microsoft Office include the replacement of the standard menu and tool-bars with a new graphical interface called Ribbon. Now, to get to the "File" menu, you have to click on an Office 2007 button. The Ribbon was designed to make features of the application more discoverable and accessible with fewer mouse clicks. Live Preview allows the user to temporarily apply formatting to an object and preview the appearance of the changes before actually applying them. The new "Mini Toolbar" is a menu that displays when text is selected. This toolbar provides access to the most commonly used formatting tools, eliminating the need to right-click.

One of the most important changes with Microsoft Office 2007 is the file format change. Microsoft Office 2007 uses a new file format called Office OpenXML as the default file format. It is based on the XML and ZIP file format, and allows for documents created in this format to be 50 to 75 percent smaller in size than they would be if saved in the previous file formats used in older versions of Microsoft Office. Microsoft Office Applications can be set up to save in formats previously used in older versions of Microsoft Office. For example, Microsoft Word 2007 can be configured to save document files using the ".doc" file extension rather than the new ".docx" extension. This allows users with older versions of the software to open and view documents created with Microsoft Word 2007. The same can be done for all of the Office programs.

If the default file format is not changed, users who have older versions of Microsoft Office will have to download a compatibility pack from Microsoft's Web site to open and view files created with Microsoft Office 2007 programs. This is the chief complaint we hear from our non-Office 2007 clients. You may run into this problem if you receive an e-mail attachment that was created using Microsoft Word 2007 and you are currently using Microsoft Word 2000 or 2003. You can just Google "Office 2007 File Converters" or to make things easier for you, at the following URLs, you can download the compatibility pack.

http://www.microsoft.com/downloads/details.aspx?FamilyId= 941B3470-3AE9-4AEE-8F43-C6BB74CD1466&displaylang=en or **http://tinyurl.com/y5a879**

Corel Suite

WordPerfect Office X4 is the latest version of Corel's Office Suite and is available in both Standard and Professional Editions for the business user. WordPerfect Office X4 was released in April 2008, and is the successor to WordPerfect Office X3. The components of WordPerfect Office X4 Standard Edition include:

WordPerfect X4—word processor

QuattroPro X4—spreadsheet application

Presentations X4—presentation/slide show creator

Corel Visual Intelligence SE—data analysis tool

WordPerfect Lightning—digital notebook

WordPerfect MAIL—e-mail client

Professional Edition does not include WordPerfect MAIL but includes the Paradox database management program and the WordPerfect Office Software Development Kit, both of which are not included in the Standard Edition.

The Standard Edition would be the version best suited for serving the solo or small firm needs. Unless you're going to need to use a database application, there is no reason for a solo or small firm to invest in the Professional Edition. Some of the new features of Corel WordPerfect Office X4 include support for Microsoft Office 2007 documents as well as for new open standards like OOXML and ODF. It also provides suite-wide PDF capabilities that will allow you to create documents, spreadsheets, and presentations in PDF format without spending hundreds of dollars on a license for Adobe Acrobat, although we highly recommend Acrobat 8 or 9 Professional for a law office. An enhanced metadata removal feature is included that will allow you to remove hidden confidential information from your documents and a new redaction tool that allows you to replace sensitive and confidential information.

One of the advantages of WordPerfect over Microsoft Word is the Reveal Codes option, which allows users to manage documents formatting with a fine tooth comb. Service and support for Corel WordPerfect X4 is a bargain when compared to the costs of support for Microsoft Office 2007. Users can request help via e-mail for free, and a toll-free support number is also provided costing users only $15 per incident. For those who want to look for help themselves, Corel has a thorough online knowledgebase that can be searched and reviewed for free.

Even with the new features included with WordPerfect Office X4, we still prefer the more seamless, although imperfect, Microsoft Office 2007. Corel has priced the software suite at a much-reduced cost when compared to Microsoft Office, particularly for business-friendly packages. Users who don't need all of the extensive features might opt instead to use a product such as OpenOffice, which is free.

Corel WordPerfect Office X4 Standard Edition costs $299 for the full license and $199 for the upgrade license. Professional Edition costs $399 for the full license and $259 for the upgrade license.

Open Office

Open Office is a free software office suite that is available for many different operating systems including Linux, Windows and Mac OS X. The latest release of OpenOffice version 3.0.0 was released in October of 2008, and contains many features and functionality that is present in other office suites such as Microsoft Office and Corel WordPerfect

Office. This suite was developed to reduce the dominating market share that Microsoft Office has by providing a free, open and high-quality alternative.

OpenOffice can read and write most of the file formats found in Microsoft Office, including Office 2007 file formats, which is important if you are going to choose to use a free utility for your productivity software. It also natively supports the standard OpenDocument file formats (ODF), and has the capability to read WordPerfect Office, Rich Text Format, Lotus and other common productivity file types. The goal of OpenOffice was to provide the public with an office productivity suite that had improved performance, speed, less memory consumption, greater scripting capabilities, better interoperatability with Microsoft Office and improved overall usability.

The components of OpenOffice work closely together to provide the features expected from a modern office suite and include:

Writer—word processor

Calc—spreadsheet application

Impress—presentation program

Base—database program

Draw—an editor used for drawing

Math—allows for creating and editing mathematical formulas

All of the components of the OpenOffice suite look and feel like the corresponding components in Microsoft Office and Corel WordPerfect Office. Microsoft, seeing the need for and popularity of the open source movement, has sponsored the development of a converter from Office Open XML to OpenDocument format and vice-versa. Microsoft and Corel have included add-in support for the ODF file format into their office suite products to allow reading and writing to the format.

Some of the new features included in the latest version of the software include:

—Personal Information Manager

—PDF import into Draw

—OOXML support for opening documents created in Microsoft Office 2007

—Extensions, to add third-party functionality

—Support for multiscreen presentations

However much we all grimace at Microsoft's domination, we do not recommend that you use OpenOffice as your primary productivity suite. Since the software is developed and maintained by freelance programmers and other companies whom make contributions to the project such as IBM and Sun, the software is not very well supported and may not contain all of the features provided by other productivity suites. In addition, most law office staff have never seen OpenOffice so the learning curve would be pretty steep.

The current release of OpenOffice can be downloaded from their web site free of charge at **www.openoffice.org**.

Adobe Acrobat

Adobe Acrobat is a family of application software developed by Adobe Systems, and uses Adobe's Portable Document Format (PDF) as its native file format. The latest version, Adobe Acrobat 9, was released in July 2008.

New features included in the latest version include the ability to embed FLV or H.264 video in PDF files for direct playback in Acrobat or Acrobat Reader, enhanced capabilities to capture Web pages to PDF and the ability to use **Acrobat.com** online services with the software to store and share files online, facilitating collaboration with other users. Signing up for the online community is free. It offers its users 5 GB of storage space, and contains many useful online services such as file sharing and storage, PDF converter, online word processor and Web conferencing. Users can sign up at **www.adobe.com**.

Acrobat 9 also includes the ability to handle dynamic maps, enhanced 256-bit encryption and improved forms and redaction capabilities. The software allows users to convert eight formats, including MOV and WMV files to Flash content that can be embedded within PDFs along with audio.

Adobe Acrobat 9 Professional Edition contains all of the same useful tools for legal professionals that were introduced in version 8, which include:

- Redaction
- Metadata removal
- Built-in support for Bates numbering

♦ Accurate exporting to Microsoft Word

♦ Improved OCR engine

♦ Enable forms saving in Adobe Reader 8

♦ New user interface

♦ Support for PDF/A archiving standard

♦ Faster Adobe PDF creation

♦ Created Adobe PDF Packages

The redaction and metadata removal tools can help mitigate the risk of unintended disclosure of information while submitting legal documents to clients, opposing counsel or the courts. Bates numbering is a method of applying identifying labels to a set of related documents, where each page is assigned a sequential Bates number that uniquely identifies it while also establishing its relationship to other Bates-numbered pages.

Adobe Acrobat 9 allows you to combine multiple documents to create an Adobe PDF package, while retaining the properties of the individual documents. Using Adobe PDF package, legal professionals can associate related project or client files, while individual files in the package can be encrypted, digitally signed, rearranged, removed or added so that each recipient of the package can read or access only the relevant files that they have permission to view.

On a side note, using Adobe Acrobat for e-mail archiving is a great way to keep your mailbox clean and in some ways is a better, easier-to-use solution than the archaic built-in archiving solution provided in Outlook. If you have Adobe Acrobat installed, then you probably have seen the toolbar added to your Outlook window with a bunch of new options. The most useful option for archiving, "Convert Selected Folder to PDF," is a powerful tool. It's straightforward and simple. Just select the folder within Outlook that you wish to archive and click on this button. A progress bar will appear and display the status of the archiving process, creating a single searchable PDF containing all of the e-mails in the selected folder. The PDF file contains a convenient bookmarked list that hyperlinks to the referenced e-mail message—a great way to quickly locate specific messages. Even attachments are included. If e-mail has an attachment, click on the attachment hyperlink within the PDF file and the attachment will open in the appropriate application. The consolidated PDF file is searchable by Sender, Subject, and Date. This is a great way to keep your mailbox clean and small. Your IT staff will love you for this.

Even with all of the new features contained within version 9, we are not as excited about this release as we were with version 8. Here is our recommendation: If you're currently using Adobe Acrobat 7.0 or earlier, then the upgrade is a must. The software contains added features for legal professionals that were unavailable in earlier versions of Acrobat and those features alone are worth the purchase and use of Adobe Acrobat 9 Professional Edition.

Adobe Acrobat 9 Pro Extended version includes Adobe Presenter, Adobe LifeCycle Designer ES and Adobe 3D Reviewer software. Adobe Acrobat 9 Pro Extended contains all of the features included in the Professional Edition, plus the ability to easily add audio and video to presentation slides to create rich, interactive presentations with Adobe Presenter, convert 2D and 3D CAD designs to PDF for cross-platform sharing and collaboration, and the ability to create 3D PDF maps. For the added cost ($200), the Pro Extended version is not the best choice for attorneys.

If you're using Adobe Acrobat 8 Professional Edition, then we would not recommend the upgrade now. The added features contained in version 9 are not by themselves worth the cost to upgrade, and we would recommend that you continue to use Acrobat 8 until we see what the next release has in store for us.

Adobe Acrobat 9 Professional Edition can be purchased online from Adobe's Web site (**www.adobe.com**) or from your local electronics store for $449 for the Full Version, or $159 if upgrading from a previous version of Acrobat.

Adobe Acrobat 9.0
Professional Edition

OCR Software

Optical Character Recognition (OCR) software translates graphical images into editable text. This capability is used most commonly when you need to edit a scanned document or image. OCR software will translate the image to editable text, such as a Microsoft Word document.

OmniPage Professional 16, by Nuance Communications, Inc., is an optical character recognition software product enabling the conversion of paper documents and TIFF files to a text-based format, for amending as needed with prominent business communications software. OmniPage Professional 16 can convert scanned images to Microsoft Word, Excel, Corel WordPerfect, Lotus 123, e-mail and HTML. The program generates a formatted text document that preserves the layout format, character, font and style of the original scanned image. The software boasts a 50% greater accuracy than its competitors when converting, and the updated recognition dictionaries for financial, legal, and medical specialties allow for legal specific word recognition. This capability means that you'll spend less time editing your legal documents.

OmniPage now supports data capture from a digital camera. The software can OCR a digital photograph, which may come in handy for attorneys who use photographs as exhibits. This software is the first OCR application designed for the multi-core processor computer, taking advantage of hyper-threading to increase the conversion speed of documents. It also is the first OCR software to support Microsoft Office 2007 native formats. When converting legal documents, OmniPage now has a greater ability to recognize formatting such as line numbers, date stamps, signatures, and more. OmniPage Professional 16 can be purchased online from Nuance's Web site (**www.nuance.com**) for $499.99 for the Full version and $199.99 for the Upgrade version.

Nuance OmniPage
Professional 16

Adobe Acrobat has an OCR engine, too. We recommend purchasing Acrobat first to see if it meets your OCR needs before expending funds on another product like OmniPage.

Voice Recognition Software

Arguably one of the biggest recent advances in productivity software is the recent improvement to voice recognition software. Dragon Naturally Speaking 10 by Nuance (**www.nuance.com**) has finally made voice recognition software a respectable addition to your productivity arsenal. Many solos and small firm lawyers are now using Dragon as their primary composition tool. This is especially valuable for those who aren't very good typists. It only takes a short period of time to train Dragon to your voice and its accuracy is astonishing.

A key component to the success of voice recognition is the use of a good quality USB microphone headset. We have had great success using a Plantronics 510 headset/microphone system, but they're no longer manufactured. The Plantronics 625 is available for $45 from the Plantronics Web site (**www.plantronics.com**) and should be a good replacement for the older 510 model.

Dragon can be used to compose e-mail messages, draft documents in your word processor, and even launch software applications without touching the keyboard or mouse. The software now allows users to search the Web and their computers through the use of voice shortcuts.

This is a great tool for handicapped individuals and used by many with disabilities. But make no mistake—this is a mainstream product and the able-bodied are moving to this technology in hordes!

Dragon Naturally Speaking comes in several versions. We recommend using the Legal or Professional versions if you can afford it. The Legal version contains vocabulary specific to the legal profession. The Professional version is a higher end package that allows for roaming user profiles and allows multiple custom dictionaries. The Professional version costs over $650 and may be purchased from many online stores. The Preferred package costs around $200 and may be a good alternative for some attorneys, as it supports digital recording devices, smart formatting and text-to-speech. Dragon Naturally Speaking 10 is licensed on a per-user basis. You can install and run it on multiple computers, but you need a license for each user's voice file that will be used.

The most important tip about using voice recognition software is to proof any output from Dragon. The speech to text is darn good and it "learns" and improves with time, but it's not perfect either. Make sure you proofread your documents, especially those that may be submitted to the court.

If you use Dragon on multiple computers, make sure you know how to move your voice files among machines. This will save on the "retraining" time when you use several computers. The process is most appropriate for those lawyers who use a computer at home and one at the office. Moving the voice files between the machines allows you to take advantage of the aggregate training time instead of each machine being seen as a stand-alone operation.

Nuance Dragon
Naturally Speaking 10

CHAPTER TEN

Security Software

COMBINED WITH NETWORK FIREWALLS or IDS devices, security software is another line of defense against malware, Trojan horses, and worms. These threats can be extremely harmful to a corporate network and extremely costly to remove once an infection has occurred. In a solo or small firm network, your client data is of the utmost importance and securing your computers, servers, and data should be taken seriously. Below, the top anti-virus, anti-spyware, anti-spam and firewall software for stand-alone computers are discussed with recommendations regarding the software's set-up and configuration.

Stand-Alone

The software applications described in the stand-alone section are primarily for the computers and laptops of solo practitioners.

Anti-virus Protection

AVG Anti-Virus from Grisoft offers premium protection against viruses, worms, Trojans, and unwanted programs for both home and business computers. The virus scanning engine has won numerous awards for its excellent detection rate, and the program offers features to help keep your business computer safe. One of those features is the full-on access protection which will automatically scan each and every file a user opens, executes, or saves. If the file is infected, the software will prevent it from being accessed, thus preventing the threat's execution. The system scanning process is automated and can be set up with flexible scheduling to meet any user's needs. The software includes more than just anti-virus protection for your system. The integrated protection also includes anti-spyware, anti-rootkit, and a Web shield that protects your system from malicious Web sites.

The anti-virus software offers full e-mail protection scanning every e-mail sent or received for viruses and threats. AVG Anti-Virus supports the most commonly used e-mail clients such as Microsoft Outlook, Microsoft Outlook Express, Eudora, and all other SMTP/POP e-mail clients. With the purchase of the software, the program will update itself automatically when program and definition updates are released without user intervention required. AVG Anti-Virus software supports the Microsoft 98/ME/NT/2000/XP/Vista operating systems. The purchase of a license for this product comes with free 24/7 e-mail technical support and free up-to-the-minute updates as they are released. AVG Anti-Virus can be purchased from Grisoft's Web site (**www.grisoft.com**) for $34.99 (one-year subscription) or $51.99 (two-year subscription).

Many attorneys mistakenly think that they can download and use the free version of AVG Anti-Virus. The license agreement for the free version only allows for personal use on a home computer. It's very clear that you may not use the free version on your law office computers or in a commercial setting. This includes the home offices of solo practitioners!

AVG Anti-Virus

Anti-spyware Protection

Webroot Spy Sweeper 5.8 has constantly been the highest rated anti-spyware solution in recent years. The software's latest version has simplified the program's configuration settings and completely revamped its interface. Spy Sweeper 5.8 now has fewer popup warnings and has additional layers of security features to specifically target devious keylogger utilities and malicious programs that use rootkit techniques to hide.

Spy Sweeper's various "shields" provide active protection to keep spyware from invading a clean system. What's more, the program can be set up to automatically check for program and spyware definition updates, automatic start-up, or scheduled scans, almost eliminating the need for user interaction. A spyware scan should be set to scan automatically at least three days a week. This is a good recommendation for the need to regularly scan a system without being paranoid. While a system is being scanned for spyware, you may notice a slowdown in system performance. This is not uncommon with anti-virus and anti-spyware scans.

This version of Spy Sweeper is compatible with Windows Vista. Webroot offers free customer support to their customers who can submit a support request online or call technical support at no cost. A one-year subscription for Webroot Spy Sweeper version 5.8 can be purchased and downloaded from Webroot's Web site (**www.webroot.com**) for $29.95. This software product is offered for purchase with one-, two-, or three-year subscriptions.

Webroot Spy Sweeper 5.8

Anti-spam Protection

Everyone hates getting spam in their e-mail in-boxes, as it takes time to go through to determine whether some clever message is spam or not. Certainly no one wants to lose a legitimate message from a client. The average user must spend at least a few minutes a day checking his or her spam folders. For the stand-alone computer, we recommend a product from Sunbelt-Software called iHateSpam.

iHateSpam has been voted the best spam filter client for the past couple of years. iHateSpam works with Microsoft Outlook and Microsoft Outlook Express, including Outlook 2007. The software eliminates irritating junk mail and phishing attempts, and will not let you lose valid e-mail messages. It stores all e-mail flagged as spam in a Quarantine folder until the user decides to delete its contents. Since spam is constantly changing and updating, iHateSpam automatically checks for updates to its spam filters when you start your e-mail program and installs them

Sunbelt-Software's IHateSpam

automatically. There is no user interaction required to update the definitions. A one-year subscription to iHate-Spam can be purchased from Sunbelt-Software's Web site (**www.sunbelt-software.com**) for $19.95. Remember that this is a stand-alone product that specifically deals with spam. You may want to consider products that provide multiple functions instead of just a single anti-spam product.

Integrated Protection

Solos and small firms may want to consider a single integrated product to deal with spam, viruses and malware. Norton's security suite is a top seller for the single computer market. We highly recommend avoiding the Symantec Norton Internet Security 2009 software. We have found it to be a heavy load on computer processing and it causes stability problems with many programs. It is also on the expensive side. We recommend instead using Kaspersky Internet Security 2009, which contains firewall, anti-virus, anti-spyware, rootkit detection, anti-spam and much more. Kaspersky is available directly from the Web site, **www.kaspersky.com**, and costs $79.95 for one year of protection on up to three computers. This is an excellent choice for the small-office environment.

Enterprise Versions

Enterprise versions of anti-virus, anti-spyware, and anti-spam software are designed for small, medium and large computer networks, and the software administration is performed from the server. The client software is installed or pushed from the server to the local workstations. The server supplies the clients with program and definition updates and will provide an interface to centrally manage all clients from a single location. Of course, enterprise licenses are a little bit more costly than just purchasing a single license.

Anti-virus Protection

Kaspersky Business Space Security protects both Window and Linux-based servers (including 64-bit versions) from all types of malicious programs and threats. The product provides protection from threats such as viruses, Trojans, worms, keystroke loggers, malware, rootkits, bots, etc. This is a new direction that we are seeing in the security product market. The anti-virus vendors are beginning to provide protection for malware, and the anti-spyware vendors are beginning to integrate anti-virus capabilities.

The anti-virus software provides real-time protection by scanning all files that are opened and quarantines infected files. The application can scan specified areas of the file system based on scheduled scans or upon demand from the administrator. The scanning of critical system areas such as running processes and startup objects helps prevent malicious code from launching.

Kaspersky Anti-Virus software is a scalable anti-virus solution, allowing administrators to define the number of instances of the program they would like to run simultaneously to accelerate the processing of server requests. The software offers flexible administration through centralized installation and control. The administration tool can be used to centrally install and manage client applications and to push updates to the clients once they are downloaded and installed for rapid deployment of critical security updates.

Kaspersky Anti-Virus, similar to other integrated security solutions, not only scans for viruses but also other threats and pests such as spyware. In most instances this solution can serve multiple functions. We use this security solution on our network systems to provide us with anti-virus and anti-spyware protection. By using an integrated solution that is capable of handling both anti-virus and anti-spyware protection, that is one less product we have to purchase and renew each year.

There is a 10-license minimum purchase for Kaspersky Business Space Security software. Cost for the product begins at $35 per license and includes technical support and upgrades for a year. Kaspersky is priced much lower per license than its competition and is an affordable, complete security solution that is taking over the market. This software product is offered for purchase with one, two-, or three-year subscriptions.

Licenses can be obtained directly from Kaspersky's Web site (**www .kaspersky.com**).

Besides Kaspersky, we also recommend using the Enterprise product from Trend Micro. Symantec has fallen from favor, especially since the introduction of its Symantec Endpoint Protection product. We have been converting clients away from Symantec since experiencing significant performance and stability problems. Worst-case situations include servers going into deadlock conditions for absolutely no reason. Miraculously, the servers function properly after Symantec is uninstalled. We had so many issues with this product that we have entirely forsaken it—and yes, this is a brand new and disturbing development.

Trend Micro Worry-Free Business Security is a highly regarded product that is available in two editions, Standard and Advanced. Both editions include anti-virus and anti-spyware capabilities. The software will protect both your servers and computers from malicious threats, and will automatically change settings on laptops to set for protection of employees when they are out of the office. The software will monitor active processes and applications to prevent unauthorized and harmful changes to your computer. Unlike the Standard Edition, the Advanced Edition includes anti-spam filtering for Microsoft Exchange Servers as well as InterScan Messaging Hosted Security. Cost for the product starts at around $38 per license for the Standard Edition and $60 per license for the Advanced Edition, which includes technical support and upgrades for a year. This software product is offered in both one- and two-year subscriptions and licenses can be purchased directly from Trend Micro's Web site (**www.trendmicro.com**).

Anti-spyware Protection

If you choose not to purchase an integrated security solution to protect your network from viruses and threats, and opt to buy each component independently, then you should consider Webroot for your anti-spyware protection needs. However, we strongly recommend considering purchasing an integrated security solution for your network, which will save your firm a lot of time and money in terms of license costs, set-up and configuration, and in solutions management.

Webroot AntiSpyware Corporate Edition 3.5 protects your network from dangerous and costly spyware attacks. The software offers centralized and flexible management, active directory integration for simplified network installation and deployment, enhanced proactive real-time threat protection capabilities, powerful spyware detection, and seamless integration with existing security applications. It also has a minimal impact on desktop performance while running. Webroot AntiSpyware is Windows Vista compatible and has the scalability to serve thousands of desktops in a network environment. Webroot AntiSpyware Corporate Edition 3.5 (formally Webroot Spy Sweeper Enterprise Edition) is a centrally managed, scalable enterprise solution that provides best-of-breed protection against all types of malicious spyware, adware, and other harmful intruders.

Webroot AntiSpyware Corporate Edition comprehensively detects and removes existing spyware and blocks new threats before your employees can unwittingly infect their computers. In light of the failure of employees to practice safe computing, protecting your employees from themselves is not a bad idea. The cost to remove spyware from an infected machine can be rather expensive and, sometimes, with the cleverest spyware, you cannot be sure that it's been completely removed. To prevent these unnecessary costs, it's strongly recommended that you protect your system from spyware and other malicious threats in combination with anti-virus protection.

The software can be purchased online from Webroot's Web site for around $20 per license for a one-year subscription. This software product is offered for purchase with one-, two-, or three-year subscriptions.

Anti-spam Protection

Symantec Mail Security 6.0 for Microsoft Exchange provides high-performance, integrated mail protection against virus threats, spam, and security risks while enforcing internal policies on Microsoft Exchange servers. The software is compatible with Microsoft Exchange 2000/2003/2007 servers.

The software has advanced anti-virus protection with updates approximately every 30 minutes, and boasts a catch rate of up to 97 percent of all spam messages. You will need to purchase the Premium AntiSpam option to provide spam protection. The software defends against new and known viruses and security risks for superior virus protection. It further allows you to filter inappropriate content within most file formats while preventing inappropriate communications. The software is centrally managed and flexible, allowing you to create different rules based on user or group.

On the client workstation, a Symantec Antispam toolbar is installed that allows users to tag spam messages that get through the filter as spam, which will remove the messages from the in-box to the designated spam folder. All messages tagged as spam are moved to a spam folder and remain present in the folder until the user deletes them. This allows the user to discover false positives before clearing the spam messages from the system. The software is easy to install and configure, and provides great spam protection.

The Symantec Mail Security for Microsoft Exchange software can be purchased online from Symantec's Web site for roughly $30 per license for a one-year subscription. It is highly recommended that when purchasing licenses for Symantec Mail Security, you should buy Symantec Brightmail Premium AntiSpam licenses as well. A one-year license subscription for Symantec Brightmail Premium AntiSpam is roughly $25 per license, which can also be purchased online from Symantec's Web site. The combination of Symantec Mail Security and the Premium AntiSpam products make this solution rather expensive just to get anti-spam protection; however, it is arguably the most effective anti-spam solution currently available and keeps you in control of your data.

A lower cost alternative is to use the Postini service for e-mail anti-spam and anti-virus. Note that your e-mail flow will be re-routed so that it goes through the Postini servers before being delivered to your mail server or e-mail client. You can purchase the Postini service directly or go through a reseller. When you purchase directly, the costs are lower, but you have to configure and setup the installation yourself and you do not receive any support. Purchasing through a reseller costs slightly more money, but you obtain 24/7 support and assistance with the complete operation. Postini provides a Web-based interface to manage the quarantine, where spam messages are held. Postini has a very good reputation for quality service and clients seem to be very happy with it.

CHAPTER ELEVEN

More about
Macs. . . .

APART FROM THE INFORMATION conveyed previously about Mac laptops and desktops, we want to offer you additional data in light of the
recent interest attorneys have shown in potentially switching to Macs.
Most attorneys have never used a Mac, either in their personal life or for
their job. Some people argue that Macs are ready for "prime time," to take
on Windows-based PCs in the business place. From a hardware stand-
point, Macs are just as good, if not better than PCs. You can't really tell
them apart anymore since Macs made the switch to using Intel-based
processors. The only difference now is the operating system, which is still
the main obstacle for Macs gaining a greater piece of the pie in the business marketplace.

Frankly, the problem lies with software compatibility with Macs. Most law
firms, no matter the size, use legal specific software on a daily basis to do
their jobs. Whether it's case management, billing, trial-related or field-spe-
cific, most vendors of specialized software don't make versions for Macs.
But for attorneys who use a computer just for word processing, Internet
research, filing motions, billing and accounting, a Mac could suit you just
fine. Below, we discuss some Mac-specific hardware and software solutions
that may come in handy if you are or want to become a Mac user.

Hardware

AirPort Extreme

Apple's AirPort Extreme is their wireless solution for home, school, and
business networks. The wireless router plugs directly into your cable or DSL

modem and connects users wirelessly to the Internet. This router supports the 802.11a/b/g protocols, along with the draft 802.11n standard. The wireless router supports NAT, DHCP and VPN passthrough, allowing users the capability of connecting to their office network from home. The AirPort Extreme comes with built-in security features such as a NAT firewall, WiFi Protected Access, WPA/WPA2 and WEP encryption and MAC address filtering. The router contains one Gigabit Ethernet WAN port for connecting to a cable or DSL modem, and three Gigabit Ethernet LAN ports for connecting computers or networking devices. The built-in USB is provided to connect a printer or hard drive to be shared to users on the local network.

Apple's AirPort Extreme

The AirPort Extreme is both Mac and Windows compatible and comes bundled with software, power cord and documentation. The AirPort Extreme can be purchased directly online from the Apple Store (**store.apple.com**) for $179.

AirPort Express

The AirPort Express Base Station is a portable wireless router, perfect for taking with you on the road. The small wireless router is extremely portable, about the size of a postcard and weights less than 7.5 ounces. The router supports the 802.11a/b/g protocols, along with the draft 802.11n standard. This wireless device is great for hotels, supplying your laptop with wireless Internet so you can surf from any location in the room. The device has a built-in USB port for connecting a shared printer, and an Ethernet port for connecting to your DSL and cable modem or your local network. The built-in wireless security supports WPA/WPA2, WEP, NAT and MAC address filtering. The AirPort Express Base Station is both Mac and Windows compatible and comes bundled with the software needed to get your computer connected to the wireless network. The AirPort Express Base Station can be purchased directly online from the Apple Store (**store.apple.com**) for $99.

Apple's AirPort Express Base Station with 802.11n and AirTunes

Time Capsule

Looking for a solution to automatically back up your files? Time Capsule works seamlessly with Time Machine, backup software included with the Mac OS X Leopard operating system. Time Capsule is a wireless router with a built-in hard drive used for storing backups of your files. Using the

Time Machine backup software, the application will back up your files and folders automatically, without user intervention. The data is backed up over the local wireless network to the Time Capsule hardware device. Time Capsule can be purchased and used solely as a backup solution, or it can also provide wireless Internet connectivity to your local network. It has the same built-in features and functionality as the AirPort Extreme.

Time Capsule is offered in two models, with storage capacities of 500 GB and 1 TB. The Time Capsule can be purchased directly online from the Apple Store (**store.apple.com**) starting at $299.

Apple's Time Capsule

Apple Cinema Display

The Apple Cinema Display is a model line of high definition (HD) flat panel LCD monitors offered in sizes of 20", 23", and 30" of diagonal viewing area. Its wide screen format makes this monitor a perfect display for legal professionals, providing enough real estate to display two or

Apple Cinema HD Display

more documents side-by-side. The display accepts DVI inputs and is compatible with both Windows and Mac computers. The monitor has a 700:1 contrast ratio, 14 ms response time and a screen coated with an anti-glare substance. The monitor has two USB 2.0 and two FireWire 400 ports to connect peripherals and can be purchased with an optional VESA wall mount. The Apple Cinema Display can be purchased directly online from the Apple Store (**store.apple.com**) starting at $599.

Apple Wireless Keyboard

The Apple Wireless Keyboard uses Bluetooth wireless technology, eliminating the need for obstructive and unfriendly wires to connect your keyboard to your computer. The wireless keyboard comes in a low-profile, anodized aluminum frame that matches the Apple theme seamlessly. The keyboard contains function keys for one-touch access to Mac features, and has power management features to conserve the battery when not in use. The Apple Wireless Keyboard requires Mac OS X version 10.4.10 or later and takes three AA batteries. The Apple Wireless Keyboard can be purchased directly online from the Apple Store (**store.apple.com**) for $79.

Apple Wireless Keyboard

Apple Wireless Mighty Mouse

Like the Apple Wireless Keyboard, the Mighty Mouse uses Bluetooth wireless technology to connect the mouse to your computer. The laser tracking allows you to use the mouse on a number of surfaces, while maintaining the precision and accuracy of tracking movement. The mouse uses touch-sensitive technology to detect both right and left clicks, and the innovative scrolling ball allows for 360-degree scrolling capabilities. The mouse can be powered with either one or two AA batteries, and when paired with the Apple wireless keyboard, allows you to work wire free at your desk. The Apple Wireless Mighty Mouse can be purchased directly online from the Apple Store (**store.apple.com**) for $69.

Apple Wireless
Mighty Mouse

Software

Microsoft Office 2008 for Mac

We often are asked, "Can I open Microsoft Office documents on a Mac computer?" The short answer is yes. Microsoft Office 2008 for Mac is the answer. This Microsoft product is the latest version of the productivity suite for the Mac platform. Microsoft Office 2008 includes Microsoft Word, Microsoft Excel, Microsoft PowerPoint, Microsoft Entourage and Microsoft Messenger, all for the Mac computer. Microsoft Word, Excel and PowerPoint are compatible with their Windows counterparts. Microsoft Entourage is like Microsoft Outlook, an e-mail client for Macs. Entourage includes support for Microsoft Exchange Server (2000/2003/2007), so getting your corporate e-mail on your Mac is no longer an issue.

Microsoft Office 2008 for Macs requires Mac OS X version 10.4.9 or later, and is available in both a Standard and Upgrade Edition. Microsoft Office 2008 can be purchased online from the Apple Store (**store.apple.com**) for $239.95 for the Upgrade Edition and $399.95 for the Standard Edition.

Microsoft Office
2008 for Mac

Toast 9 Titanium by Roxio

Toast 9 Titanium is the latest version of Roxio's long running disc-burning software for the Mac. With this software you can burn video or data to CDs or DVDs. New to this version is the ability to burn high-definition video to Blu-ray and HD-DVD. Toast even allows a user to capture streaming audio from any Web site, and then to transfer the audio to your iPod. The software has built-in basic features such as the ability to compress, convert, and compile video in most formats, along with backup software that can be scheduled to back up your data. The software can be purchased online from Roxio's Web site (**www.roxio.com**) for $79.99.

Roxio Toast 9
Titanium

Norton Antivirus 11 for Macintosh

Want to protect your Mac computer from viruses and other threats? Norton Antivirus has an edition specifically for Mac computers that offers protection from the latest viruses and threats. Norton Antivirus 11 is compatible with OS X v 10.4.10 systems and newer, and runs natively on Intel and PowerPC-based Mac systems. The anti-virus protection can automatically scan and clean downloaded e-mail files and attachments, and provide real-time protection and removal of viruses and other threats. Even though Macs are less susceptible to viruses and other threats they are not immune. It's still highly recommended that an anti-virus solution be used

Norton Antivirus 11
for Mac

to protect the system. Some would even be so bold as to say there are zero viruses for a Mac. Not so. There are many documented viruses that are specific to a Mac and many more that are operating system-independent. The message here is to get and install an anti-virus solution. Norton Antivirus 11 can be purchased directly from Symantec's Web site (**www.symantec.com**) for $49.95 for a one-year subscription.

Intuit Quicken 2007 for Mac/QuickBooks 2009 for Mac

Quicken for Mac offers a complete personal financial management package, providing immediate access to your accounts from a single location. By using Quicken, you can better organize your financial information and easily track your finances. Quicken 2007 provides an easy way to track and enter expenses without launching the entire application through the new QuickEntry Dashboard Widget. Quicken 2007 for Mac is the latest version of the software from Intuit that is available for purchase on its Web site. Intuit did not release a version for the Mac in 2008. Currently, Quicken 2007 for Mac is being replaced with Quicken Financial Life for Mac, still in a Beta release. Quicken 2007 for Mac can be purchased online from the Apple Store (**store.apple.com**) for $69.95.

QuickBooks, another financial and accounting package from Intuit, has an edition for Macs. QuickBooks Accounting 2009 for Macs can be used to organize your business finances. This software package can be used to track and manage your business expenses, invoicing, and payroll from a single financial application. QuickBooks for Macs can synchronize your contacts directly with the iCal program and back up data directly to your MobileMe account. This software is compatible with Mac OS X v. 10.5.4 or newer. QuickBooks Accounting 2009 for Macs can be purchased online from Intuit's QuickBooks Web site (**www.quickbooks.com**) for $199.95.

PGP Whole Disk Encryption 9.9 for Mac OS X

PGP Corporation, a leading vendor of hard disk encryption software, has released a version of its hard disk encryption suite for the Mac computer. PGP Whole Disk Encryption software provides comprehensive, non-stop disk encryption for Macs, securing data on desktops, laptops and removable devices. The encrypted data is protected from unauthorized access, requiring a user name and pass-phrase to decrypt the contents of the hard disk. PGP Whole Disk Encryption 9.9 requires Mac OS X 10.4.10 or newer.

PGP Whole Disk Encryption 9.9 for Mac OS X software can be purchased online directly from PGP's Web site (**www.pgp.com**) for $119.

CHAPTER TWELVE

Remote Access

MOST LAWYERS ARE ROAD warriors today. If their entire office is not on their laptop, a good chunk of it is—and the rest is accessible through remote access. Whether in court, on vacation, or in a meeting, lawyers need access to their e-mail, calendar, appointments, and files. Some lawyers have discarded workstations entirely, using only their laptops and a docking station at work. Others have both a workstation and a laptop. The popularity of laptops has zoomed in the last decade, to a point where the lawyer without a laptop is a relative rarity. Our new mobile lawyers are now equipped with technologies that allow them to be as productive when on the road as they are in the office, minimizing down time and keeping those billable hours up! There is a strong expectation by many clients and colleagues that lawyers will be constantly accessible via e-mail even, sadly, on vacation. We privately joke (and lament) that vacations are times when our laptops get a nice view. So how do we stay in touch with the office?

Virtual-Private Networking

A Virtual-Private Network (VPN) connection is a secure communications network tunneled through another network, such as the Internet. The VPN connection allows a network user to connect to their office when working remotely. The communications tunnel allows the data traffic between the remote user and the office network to be encrypted, to maintain the security of the information as it is passed back and forth. This is extremely important for law firms when their lawyers are working on client files while traveling or away from the office. Best of all, the VPN service software is included with Microsoft's server operating systems and the VPN client software is included with Microsoft 2000, XP, and Vista operating systems.

The typical lawyer is likely to be dumbfounded when confronted with setting up a VPN, so this is best left to your IT consultant. However, it is not terribly expensive and it offers terrific security for your data. The greatest advantage of VPNs is that they are multi-user, whereas others are one-on-one solutions.

GoToMyPC

GoToMyPC is a remote connection service that allows you to connect to your work computer when you are away from the office. This service is a great alternative if you're a solo practitioner or if your law firm can't set up a VPN-type connection for remote users (if you don't have a server). Like a VPN connection, data communications between the client and the host are encrypted and secured. In order to connect to your work computer, software must be installed and running on the host machine (the computer you wish to connect to) and both the client and the host computers must have Internet access. The GoToMyPC Web site maintains contact with the host computer so the host's IP address is always known. This is critical—the solution works even if the host's Internet connection has a dynamic Internet connection that will not remain constant. No configuration to the company firewall will need to be made to get GoToMyPC up and running.

GoToMyPC costs about $180 per year for one computer license and will need to be renewed yearly. There is no limitation on how often you may connect to your host computer, and you are not limited from which client machine you have to connect. The software requires little set-up and configuration and can be purchased online from the GoToMyPC Web site at **www.gotomypc.com**. This software is more costly than its competitors, so check out all of your available options before selecting which remote access solution to purchase.

LogMeIn

LogMeIn Pro is a remote access solution that is very similar to GoToMyPC. The software works the same way, with the service provider maintaining the IP addresses of host computers. This is a good solution for those firms with dynamic IP addresses. The service allows you to gain seamless and total access to your office PC from any computer with an Internet connection. To connect, a user logs into the LogMeIn Web site and the connection to their host computer is made automatically. Some of the features include remote printing, the ability to transfer files between the connected computers and the ability to map network drives to your local computer. Just like GoToMyPC, this service is extremely secure, using 128-to-256 bit SSL end-to-end encryption. When compared to GoToMyPC, this remote access solution costs much less. LogMeIn Pro costs $69.95 per year for one computer license, and this service subscription will need to be renewed annually. This software can be purchased online from LogMeIn's Web site at **www.logmein.com**. We strongly recommend the use of this product for remote accessibility.

Symantec pcAnywhere

Symantec pcAnywhere version 12.1 is similar to GoToMyPC, with one exception. When using pcAnywhere, you must know the host's IP address or host name in order to connect to the host computer. There is not a central database or Web site that monitors and maintains the host computer's current address. Symantec pcAnywhere works in scenarios where the host computer maintains a static IP address and will not work when the IP address is dynamically assigned. The software has many configuration options and can be set up to use encryption, file sharing, and remote printing. pcAnywhere requires more set-up and configuration than GoToMyPC does, and will require an administrator to set up port forwarding through the host's network router the client's communications can reach the destination host computer.

A license for Symantec pcAnywhere can be purchased from Symantec's Web site (**www.symantec.com/norton/symantec-pcanywhere**) or from your local electronic retail store for about $200. This software is a one-time purchase, and is not a yearly subscription, although it may need to be upgraded as updates to the software are released. The major disadvantages to using pcAnywhere are the cost, the requirement for a static IP address, and the need to install software on both ends of the communication stream. This means you won't be able to connect from the Internet café in Jamaica since you probably didn't bring your pcAnywhere CD.

Besides providing remote access solutions for the legal road warrior, we wanted to include some great tips to think about before heading out on a trip:

- Pack a surge protector—doesn't matter what brand. You never know when you will need more than two outlets to power all of your devices, and to protect your electronic devices from power surges and dirty electricity.

- Buy a lock for your laptop. Ninety-nine percent of laptops have a Kensington security slot and it's best if you use it. Kensington locks, such as the MicroSaver DS Notebook Lock, can be purchased online from Kensington's Web site (**www.kensington.com**) for around $50. A small price to pay to keep your laptop secure.

- Pack a spare cell phone charger and sync cable. You shouldn't travel without either one.

- Pack an AC extension cable. This will come in handy when you are located far away from a power outlet.

- Keep a spare AC power adapter for your laptop in your bag. You never know when you might need one.

- Pack headphones to keep the noise out. Have you ever tried to be productive on an airplane? It's hard to when the person next to you can't stop talking. Just plug in your headphones and your problem is solved. You can even listen to relaxing music while you work. For those who want wireless Bluetooth headphones, check out the Jabra BT8030 headphones, costing about $150. These wireless headphones will do the job. However, for those music aficionados, the Bose QuietComfort 3 headphones offer the top of the line in headphone technology, and include the noise-canceling circuitry that you hear everyone talking about. The downside though is the price, which is very, very expensive (about $350).

- Back up your data to an external hard drive or the network server. If your laptop crashes or is stolen, you'll want a backup of your most important files.

- Encrypt your hard drive and data. There are many software tools available to do this, such as PGP, TrueCrypt, and PC Guardian. In the event your laptop is lost or stolen, your data is protected.

These are just a few of the recommendations that we have for the legal road warriors, all based on our own experiences traveling. We've burned ourselves more than once by being ill-prepared.

CHAPTER THIRTEEN

High-Speed Internet

NONE OF OUR LAWYERS/CLIENTS ever complain that their Internet is too fast—we have almost forgotten how slow the Internet used to be and how patiently we had to wait for our screens to load. High-speed Internet is now a requirement for solos and small law firms. Fast connections have all but replaced dial-up Internet modems because of the low cost and efficiency. Why continue to wait for Web pages to load and attachments to open if you don't have to? Few creatures are more impatient than lawyers and virtually all of them have jumped to high-speed Internet within the past few years.

High-speed Internet connections are available from your local Internet Service Provider (ISP), and usually are provided over a cable, DSL, or fiber optic connection. These links offer download times in excess of 5 MB/s and varying upload speeds, depending on the provider and the service tier subscribed to. If your firm hosts its own services, such as e-mail or a Web site, static IP addresses can be obtained from your local provider with these types of connections. The ISP may charge more to issue your business a static IP address than if you just required a dynamically leased IP address. High-speed Internet access connectivity generally will cost $75–$200 per month.

If your firm requires a larger amount of bandwidth due to the number of users sharing the Internet connection or for Web-based applications, your local ISP may be able to provide a connection type that meets your requirements. Some examples of upgraded service connections are referred to as T1 or fractional T1 connections, and can cost hundreds of dollars per month. These types of connections also require longer service agreements and usually include a large set-up cost.

If available in your area, a speedy alternative to T1s is fiber optics. Fiber to the curb, such as Verizon F:OS, can offer business subscribers increasingly faster Internet connections at a much lower cost. Check with your local service providers to see if such a connection is currently available. In general, solos and small firms are well-served by cable and DSL to meet their Internet connection needs.

VoIP

It seems like the entire telecommunications world is all pumped up and wants you to buy their Voice over Internet Protocol (VoIP) service. Even the cable companies are vying for your voice services. For those who don't know, VoIP is a technology to carry voice communications over computer wires instead of the traditional fixed telephone circuits. There are exceptions to every recommendation, but generally we do not recommend that solo and small firm attorneys switch over to VoIP services. The primary reasons are reliability and security.

The entry level (re: cheap) VoIP implementations may not have all the security features available in large scale systems. As an example, call log, routing and setup information may be stored in clear text and accessible to anybody on your network. Reliability is the second issue. VoIP is dependent on the stability and quality of your Internet connection. If you have a slow or congested Internet connection, then the call quality will be terrible and sections of the conversation will drop out. You will totally lose phone service if your Internet connection is down.

A very serious issue exists with regards to 911 emergency dialing. Not all services can properly identify your location with making 911 calls. You may have to manually register your physical address every time you move your "virtual phone" to a different location.

One exception to our recommendation is using a free service such as Skype for occasional (and even international) calls. The quality is generally very good and there is no charge between Skype users.

CHAPTER FOURTEEN

Utilities

WHAT WE ALL NEED is Batman's belt, with a full repository of tricks that we can draw upon at any moment to perform the myriad of tasks associated with the practice of law. Failing that, we must acknowledge that it is impossible to list all of the utilities that a solo or small firm might find useful. There are so many great selections and just as many opinions as to what makes one utility more valuable than another.

The threshold question is, What constitutes a utility? For our purposes, we will consider a utility to be some software application that takes data and manipulates it for a specific purpose. That should allow us a lot of latitude!

The challenge is to list utilities that offer a unique purpose for the solo and small-firm lawyer. We have used many of these utilities ourselves and have had some great suggestions from our friends and colleagues. If you don't see your favorite utility here, just drop us a line and maybe it will be listed in the next edition of the book.

GreenPrint

GreenPrint Technologies (**www.printgreener.com**) has a software product, GreenPrint, which eliminates unwanted pages from your printing jobs, saving you ink, toner, paper, money, and trees. The software intercepts your print jobs and highlights unnecessary pages that can be removed, such as blank pages. How many times have you printed a Web page that prints on two pages of paper, with only a single line of text on the second page? Usually the second page contains only a URL, logo, or banner ad. No longer will these wasted pages need to be printed.

GreenPrint makes recommendations about pages that should be removed from the print job and prompts the user for approval before sending the job to the printer. The software tracks the number of pages and costs it has saved—a great feature for the cost-conscious. There is a free edition of the software for home use and an Enterprise Edition for businesses. The Enterprise Edition costs $70 per license, with volume discounts available for larger orders.

Winscribe for the Legal Profession

Winscribe, a leading developer of dictation software, has a made a product specifically for the legal profession that allows dictations to be automatically transcribed, converting recorded words to text. Automating the process saves both time and money, increasing the efficiency of your employees. End of the listen . . . type era. Now your employees can spend their time doing something more productive and billable. Winscribe can even integrate with existing applications, such as your document management system, thereby streamlining your workflow process.

Another innovative feature of this software is that it supports a wide range of input from recordings made on telephones, PCs and laptops, digital handheld devices, PDAs, and even BlackBerrys. The days of carrying around a digital recorder may be over. Now you can install mobile software on your smartphone to record dictations and transfer the files wirelessly to your firm network. As always, client confidentiality is an extremely important issue. Winscribe protects dictations through the encryption of the files and through implementing a secure file-transfer process. Winscribe has been vetted by the experts and found worthy. This product is available on Winscribe's Web site at **www.winscribe.com**.

YouSendIt

What a wonderful resource to transmit large file attachments without charge. There are several service packages, with one being free. The free offering is called Lite and can transmit an attachment that is up to 100 MB in size. Since a lot of ISPs limit the size of attachments, YouSendIt is a great alternative to "push" the occasional large attachment. The service works by creating an account at **yousendit.com** and actually uploading the file to the YouSendIt service. You provide the e-mail addresses for the recipient(s), and an e-mail message is sent with a hyperlink that allows for the download of the file from the YouSendIt site. If you need to regularly transmit very large attachments, especially those larger than 100 MB, YouSendIt provides several pay services to accomplish this. The paid services provide enhancements, such as e-mail support, longer availability for file downloads, and more bandwidth for downloads. We have found this resource to be invaluable for sending conference attendees copies of our PowerPoint presentations, which tend to be quite large because of the graphics. This terrific utility may be found at **www.yousendit.com**.

Anagram

Anagram (**www.getanagram.com**) is a piece of software that allows you to "sweep" text from an e-mail message and create a record within Outlook. You can sweep contact information that the sender has added in their message footer and instantly create an Outlook contact. The software is not just limited to the creation of contacts. You can "grab" the text and create calendar entries, to-do items, and even tasks. The text can originate from anywhere. Anagram will create the contact, calendar entry, task, etc., in your personal folder area. This is fine for most solos. If you have an Exchange Server with public folders, then the data will not go directly to the public folder. You will have to move it from your personal folder if the intended destination is a public folder. Anagram is currently available for iGoogle (Gmail and Google Calendar), **Salesforce.com**, Microsoft Outlook, Netsuite, Palm Desktop, and Jigsaw. Anagram is compatible with all Windows-based systems, including Windows Vista, but not Macs.

Take address information from a Web page and create a contact. The base product costs $34.95 for a single user. There is a 45-day trial version to make sure that Anagram will work on your computer and perform according to your expectations. Make sure you download and try the trial before you spend the money; however, we're sure (especially you solo attorneys) that you'll be typing in your credit card number shortly after your first use of Anagram.

TinyURL

Have you ever wanted to give somebody a reference link only to discover that it is about 400 characters long and contains all kinds of goofy characters and non-word representations? Probably the biggest problem is the breaking up of the URL link, especially when the e-mail is viewed as text formatted. The last thing you want to do is have the recipient "cut and paste" the various parts of the URL back together. TinyURL stores the complete URL on its servers and provides a very small URL instead. The user selects the smaller TinyURL, which translates and redirects to the much larger one. This is a free service to make the posting of long URLs easier. It's available at **http://tinyurl.com**

Jott

Jott (**http://jott.com**) is a wonderful tool that is essentially a speech-to-text converter service. It's intended to be used as a quick reminder when you don't have pen and paper available. You must register in order to use the service. You begin by creating an account with your name, e-mail address, and password. Jott then sends a confirming message to the e-mail address that you entered. You will receive a link that validates your e-mail address. The next step is to register a phone number that you will use to call Jott. Normally, you would register your cell phone number as the source of the Jott message. Jott uses caller ID to validate the source of the message and tie the phone call to your user account. Obviously this won't work if you have blocked your caller ID or your provider does not transmit your caller ID to the called party. You're given a toll-free number to call Jott and complete the registration process. It's probably a good idea to create a speed dial entry on your cell phone for Jott so that you can quickly access the service.

You're allowed up to 15 seconds for each "jotted" message through Jott Basic, which is free but supported by ads. If you need more time for your "jotted" messages, then you can sign up for Jott or Jott Premium, both of which give you added features over Jott Basic. You can also import your contacts to Jott so that a message can be "jotted" to other people that you define. The one thing that we do notice is that it can take some time for the transcribed message to end up in your Inbox. Taking more than 30 minutes to deliver the message is not unusual. This means that Jott should not be used for time-sensitive communications. In addition to messages, you can Jott to links to be used as postings. As an example, you can Jott to a Yahoo! Group or Twitter with your voice.

IrfanView

Have some graphic files for that construction case that you can't seem to view? Perhaps you have a video or sound file for a wrongful termination case and don't know how to play it? IrfanView (**www.irfanview.com**) is a wonderful software application that can view a very large number of different graphic file formats and play several audio and video formats. IrfanView is compatible with all Windows-based systems, including Windows Vista. IrfanView is free for home use only, so you can't legally install it for your law practice. Even though you can technically violate the license agreement and use IrfanView, we are always on the right side of the copyright laws, and IrfanView makes it easy by charging a mere $12 to use the product in a commercial setting.

DBAN

Darik's Boot and Nuke is a free program that wipes the contents of your hard drive. DBAN is an open-source project and can be downloaded at **http://dban.sourceforge.net**. The program will automatically and permanently delete the contents of any hard disk it can detect. DBAN also allows the wiping of multiple hard disks at the same time. We all love "free," and this program is the perfect complement to any lawyer's software tool chest. You will use DBAN to wipe the data contents from your hard drives, flash drives, and floppies, making your confidential client information unrecoverable. We have all read the stories of customer data being found on hard drives purchased on eBay. Make sure that you wipe any media that may contain information you don't want someone else to recover. Could the National Security Agency recover something wiped with DBAN? Perhaps it's possible, but we've never—ever—seen evidence of it. It's free, it's safe, and it helps you comply with your ethical duty to keep your client data confidential. When you're getting ready to donate or ditch your old computers, this is an invaluable tool.

Shred 2

PC Magazine has a free utility that is designed to wipe specific files or disk areas. Shred 2 runs under Windows 95, 98, 2000, ME, NT 4.0, and XP. If you want to wipe the recycle bin, then you'll need an updated .DLL file, which is discussed in the article about Shred 2 at **www.pcmag.com/article2/0,1895,13352,00.asp**. The software can selectively wipe files or folders and can be configured to do multiple wipes of the same area if you are particularly paranoid. This utility is especially useful in removing data remnants of files and their associated file slack, which can be forensically recovered if wiping did not occur. The nice part about having a file/folder wiping utility is that data can be selectively eradicated from your computer without having to wipe the entire hard disk and having to reload the operating system and all of the applications. Remember, though, you cannot recover the file once it is wiped, so pay attention when you're clicking that mouse.

SnagIt

No lawyer should be without SnagIt. SnagIt 9 is a screen-capture utility that can capture anything on your desktop—a specific window, a defined area, an object (e.g., the title bar), or a multitude of other things. A screen-capture application is a great tool to "grab" images to place in a motion or brief that show exactly what is depicted on the computer screen. This is particularly handy when you only want a specific area of the screen. SnagIt can output the "snagged" image to a multitude of formats as well. The program costs $49.95 for a single license version, with discounts for multiple copies. There is a 30-day trial version available so you can see whether it fits your needs prior to purchase. It is available from **www.techsmith.com/screen-capture.asp** and now works on Vista.

QuickView Plus

Spend a little more money and get a utility that can view more than 300 file formats, including Microsoft Office 2007 and Corel WordPerfect Office X3. That's what you get when you purchase QuickView Plus 10. The file support comes without need of the native application. QuickView Plus maintains the formatting of the files so you can view and print files as they were originally created and meant to be seen. This is a great application to view file formats, especially from your electronic discovery cases. You can handle e-mail attachments and various "obscure" software packages that you've probably never heard of. QuickView Plus is compatible with Microsoft Windows 2000/XP/Vista systems. At $46 for a single download license, it is a perfect complement to IrfanView. QuickView Plus is available at **www.avantstar.com/Products/Quick_View_Plus/QuickViewPlus Overview**.

Sam Spade

The name of this utility, obviously, is meant to evoke Humphrey Bogart in *The Maltese Falcon*. Indeed, this utility can perform some gumshoe functions, such as troubleshooting and dealing with Internet communications. However, the most useful function of this free utility is the ability to decode e-mail headers so that the common man or woman can decipher the cryptic entries in a readable English form. Unfortunately, the original site for Sam Spade is down and no longer active. The good news is that there are several Web sites that have the current version (1.14) available for download. As we move forward into the world of electronic evidence, having the ability to decode e-mail headers is an invaluable asset to help ascertain where an e-mail "really" came from. Mind you, there are ways to hide for the world's miscreants, but Sam Spade can provide you with a lot of helpful information. Just do a Google search for "Sam Spade" and you will find several download locations on the first page of the results.

Karen's Power Tools

One of the greatest collections of utilities that we have found is a CD that contains more than 25 utilities and over 100 articles and newsletters. The CD is only $29.95 and includes a license for commercial usage. One of the most powerful programs is called Hasher. The Hasher program calculates the hash values for text strings, disk files, or group of files. Hasher can calculate the MD5, SHA-1, SHA-224, SHA-256, SHA-384, and SHA-512 hash values. This is very valuable in determining if a file or data has been changed. It is very common for the hash value to be provided along with the data file itself, thereby aiding in maintaining authenticity. You will find Hasher to be indispensable in calculating hash values for electronic evidence. For those of you who haven't the slightest clue what a hash value is, think of it as a "digital fingerprint" and you've got the basic idea. There are other valuable utilities on the CD, which can be ordered at **www.karenware.com**. All of Karen's tools are compatible with Windows-based systems, including Windows Vista.

Metadata Assistant

Our favorite metadata analysis and removal tool is Metadata Assistant by Payne Group (**www.payneconsulting.com/products/metadataretail**). Metadata Assistant integrates with your Microsoft Office installation and is particularly valuable when sending file attachments. The product will display a dialog box asking if you want to clean the attachment or just send it uncleaned. A friendly piece of advice—don't clean the metadata if you are collaborating on a document with another person, as it will remove the track changes. Metadata Assistant can also convert the attachment to PDF on the fly.

Metadata Assistant is extremely flexible and works with Word, Excel and PowerPoint versions from 97 to 2007. It has e-mail integration with Outlook 2000 to 2007, Groupwise 6.01 and higher, and Lotus Notes 5 and 6. It will integrate with Interwoven, Hummingbird, and WORLDOX document management systems. It is available directly from the Payne Group for $80 per license.

You can also remove metadata by converting the file to PDF. This does not remove all of the metadata, but does remove a large portion of it and only leaves what are typically considered innocuous values. Microsoft also has a free metadata removal tool for Office XP/2003/2007. We flatly *do not* recommend using Microsoft's tool, as it's not very effective in removing metadata. It leaves certain values behind that are still viewable by products like Metadata Assistant.

No lawyer should be without a metadata scrubber to ensure removal of potential confidential data. Some states are even addressing the removal of metadata in their ethics opinions. Whether you're required to scrub metadata or not, Metadata Assistant is an absolute "must have" utility for your practice.

Livescribe Pulse Smartpen

The Livescribe Pulse Smartpen is a device that can record a user's written notes along with the accompanying audio. The Smartpen can transmit the data to a computer via USB cable, allowing a user to view their digitalized notes and recorded audio. The pen has an infrared camera that records 72 images per second to track the spatial movement of the device on the provided sheets of dot-paper, the required use of which is one of the only downsides of the product. There are plans in the works to allow users to print their own dot paper, which would be a much-needed convenience.

Using the bundled Livescribe Desktop software, users can manage written notes and recordings, but cannot convert notes to text because the software lacks OCR capabilities. The Smartpen, just like a computer, can be updated with new firmware and software, and is currently offered with 1 or 2 GB of storage capacity. The Smartpen is compatible with Microsoft Windows XP SP2 and Vista, but currently not Macs. A pretty slick tech toy, even for those who are aren't absentminded. Now what were we about to do?

SmartDraw Legal Edition 2009

SmartDraw Legal Edition is a powerful software tool that allows attorneys to create sharp, professional-looking diagrams and trial exhibits with relative ease. It's a must have for your software arsenal. The tool, more robust than Microsoft PowerPoint, can be used to create timelines, estate planning diagrams, accident reconstruction, crime scene layouts, and more. The look and feel of the software is similar to Microsoft Office, and creating diagrams from the provided templates is simple. The Legal Edition provides specialized templates for the legal profession, over a thousand of them, and if you can't find one to use, you can create your own. Smart-Draw comes with more than 20,000 symbols and shapes to choose from, giving you the power to dynamically recreate that crucial event in your case. SmartDraw provides a number of export options, allowing users to save their work in a variety of formats such as PDF, DOC, XLS, WPD or JPG. SmartDraw Legal Edition 2009 can be purchased directly from the Web site at **www.smartdraw.com** for $297 for one user license. A trial edition is also available for download for those users who wish to test the software before purchasing.

LexisNexis' TimeMap 4

Another great timeline generating utility is LexisNexis' (previously Case-Soft) TimeMap. TimeMap is a timeline graphing tool that can be used to create polished timeline graphs for trial exhibits, presentations, and professional documents. TimeMap can be integrated with CaseMap or used on its own. Data can be directly imported into the application from Microsoft Excel, Summation, Concordance, Microsoft Access, or almost any other spreadsheet or database program, eliminating the need to manually enter data. As data is entered into the program, TimeMap will automatically generate a proportional time scale and allows the user to adjust it if necessary. Once your timeline graph has been generated, you can present the timeline using the TimeMap's Presentation Mode, or you can embed the timeline directly into your PowerPoint or Sanction presentation. TimeMap 4 includes new features such as vertical timelines, additional timeline templates, new PDF writer and enhanced integration with presentation software. TimeMap 4 supports Microsoft Windows 2000/XP or Vista, and can be purchased directly from the Web site at **www.casesoft.com**. A full-featured, 30-day trial edition is also available for download for those users who wish to give the software a test run before purchasing.

Google Desktop

Need a utility to search your files? Google Desktop is a free desktop search utility made by Google that allows a user to quickly search and located files on their computer. After installing Google Desktop, the search engine indexes the local contents of the hard drive, and upon completion allows the indexed data to be searched instantaneously. The software can index several different types of data including e-mail, Internet history, instant messaging conversations, Office documents and many other file types. The types of files that are indexed can be controlled by the user. Once the initial index has been completed, Google Desktop uses real-time indexing to add files to the index as they are opened or moved. The Google Desktop software is supported on 32-bit versions of Mac OS X, Linux and Microsoft Windows. 64-bit operating systems are not supported. Offered as a free utility, this software provides tough competition for other popular desktop search engines at no cost.

Google Desktop can be downloaded online from **http://desktop.google.com**.

X1 Professional Client

Another desktop search utility, the X1 Professional Client, allows users to search their local desktop computer for e-mail, calendars and documents. When used in conjunction with the X1 Enterprise Server and application connectors, this software can provide both network and application searching capabilities. The X1 Professional Client can index and search more than 400 file types and applications, including audio, video, e-mail files and even Internet web sites. This utility is great for searching your local computer, but if you want the ability to search your network and e-mail server, the necessary add-ins are sold separately.

A single license for the X1 Professional Client costs $50.00 and includes 1 year of technical support. Licenses can be purchased and downloaded from the X1 Technologies web site at **http://www.x1.com**.

dtSearch

Another popular desktop search engine, dtSearch, has been one of the best desktop search programs for the past 15 years. dtSearch, more powerful than Google Desktop, can index files across your local desktop computer and business network. The software provides over two dozen indexed, unindexed, fielded and full-text search options, quickly displays highlighted hits in HTML, XML or PDF format while embedding the links, formatting and images, and converts other file types to HTML format for display with highlighted search hits. The spider (*indexing agent*) can be configured with a number of options to automate the indexing process, and can even be set up to remotely index and add web sites to the searchable database. dtSearch is compatible with both 32/64-bit Linux and Windows-based computer systems.

A single license of the dtSearch 7 Desktop with Spider software costs $199, and can be purchased and downloaded from the dtSearch web site at **http://www.dtsearch.com**. Discounted prices are offered for purchases of 5 or more licenses.

CHAPTER FIFTEEN

Case Management

IF YOU STILL LIVE in the paper world, you may not know that you are probably already performing all of the functions that a case management application would provide. You are already using a Rolodex or some other type of method to aggregate your contact information. You already have a calendar to schedule events. You already have a file for each client or each client matter. We hope you already use a word processor—or at least your secretary does—to generate documents. You already track what you do for each client matter. You probably even generate some sort of status concerning each matter. These are all functions of a case management system.

It just amazes us that most solo and small firm attorneys still don't use a computerized case management software application. Case management, in our view, is essential. You may have heard other terms that describe the same type of software. Vendors attempt to differentiate themselves by describing their products with different names. You may hear descriptions such as practice management, contact management, litigation management, and so forth. Bottom line: They are all case management products, though they vary greatly in functionality.

There are several choices for case management, some of which we will cover here. The features vary by manufacturer, so make sure you understand what you're buying. Probably the most requested feature we hear is the integration of e-mail and contacts with case management. Make sure that the product will work with your e-mail system and how it's configured. The synchronization is getting better, but most of our clients are less than impressed with the current synchronization support. For example, how does the software deal with a common firm-wide public folder calendar? Will the product synchronize with your PDA or smartphone?

There are two mistakes that we consistently see when firms decide to implement a case management system. The first mistake is the failure to require everyone in the firm to use the system. You will not realize the full return on your investment if only a few employees are participating. In fact, it tends to cause a whole new set of problems because sometimes there is crossover between attorneys and cases, and yet some operate within the case management system and some do not. The second most common mistake is the failure to invest in training. Training will allow all employees to fully utilize the features of the case management system, thereby being more efficient and properly organizing all data for a client matter. Simply dumping a case management system into a firm is worse than useless. When you price the software, price the training as well.

As with other sections of this book, we cannot mention or address every case management package or every feature of every product. We mention the most popular and widely used case management packages that we see among solo and small firm attorneys.

Amicus Attorney

Amicus Attorney (**www.amicusattorney.com**) is a good small-firm package that provides a fairly simple approach to case management. The technical requirements are very reasonable and don't require a huge and expensive computer to run. There are essentially two versions available. The Small Firm Edition should work for most solo and small law firms and is recommended for up to 10 users. Pricing has not changed from last year and remains at $499 for the first user license, with each additional license costing $399.

The Premium Edition uses SQL Server 2005 to achieve unlimited user and unlimited data access. The good news is that the Premium Edition includes the required SQL CALs for SQL Server 2005 Workgroup Edition for use with Amicus Attorney, so you don't have to make a separate purchase. However, these CALs are for Amicus Attorney only and can't be used with other products. Certainly a consideration is the cost for the SQL Server software and the hardware to run it on, which can add a hefty price to the implementation costs. Like the Small Firm Edition, pricing has not changed from last year. The first user license for the premium edition costs $699, and each additional license is $599.

A welcome addition this year is the availability of Amicus Mobile, which works on your Windows Mobile (version 5 or 6) smartphone. The cost is

$149 per license and uses ActiveSync to achieve real-time, over-the-air synchronization between your phone and Amicus Attorney Premium Edition.

A trial version of Amicus Attorney is available and highly recommended if you are considering purchase. Try the product first to make sure that it meets your needs and will work in your computing environment. Amicus Attorney is often mentioned in reviews as being the most "user-friendly" product.

Time Matters

LexisNexis has a couple of offerings suitable for the solo and small firm market. Arguably the most popular case management package is Time Matters (**www.timematters.com**), but that is rapidly changing. Time Matters is a very powerful case management application, but it can also be fairly complicated for many small firm lawyers. It is an absolute necessity to purchase training if you are considering implementing Time Matters in your firm. The learning curve is steep, but well worth it because Time Matters is truly a feature-rich program.

Like most of the other case management offerings, Time Matters is sold in Professional and Enterprise versions. The former is intended for those firms that do not have so much data that they require a SQL server. The latter uses SQL Server for greater capacity. As with Amicus Attorney, the addition of SQL Server will increase your implementation costs, but does provide for a larger and more robust case management application. The Professional Edition costs $350 for the first user and $200 for each additional user. The Enterprise Edition is $700 for the first user and $400 for each additional user. A 30-day trial is available and highly recommended.

LexisNexis calls the product Lexis Front Office powered by Time Matters 9.0, although the Time Matters name alone is still used as well.

LexisNexis has a third version of Time Matters called Time Matters Browser Edition, or Lexis Front Office powered by Time Matters Browser Edition. Browser Edition is a Web-based case management system that is hosted at your firm. This edition's major advantage is its ability to access your data from any computer using the Internet and a browser. Pricing is not public and must be requested directly from LexisNexis. Additional licenses for the Browser Edition are $400 each. You can try the Browser Edition for free for up to 14 days by going to **http://testdrive.timematters.com**.

Most solo and small firms will purchase the Professional Edition of Time Matters. You can always upgrade to the Enterprise Edition if Professional doesn't scale to the volume of data in your practice. In our geographic area, it appears that more users are choosing Time Matters than any other case management software, and the users are happy—once they get past that initial learning curve! Recent efforts by LexisNexis to pressure clients into purchasing support plans have turned off many a possible client and have even caused several of our clients to abandon Time Matters altogether. The steady erosion of the Time Matters client base has caused a lot of concern, as have heavy-handed tactics from Lexis-Nexis selling support for the product. Some consultants are predicting the eventual demise of Time Matters, feeling that Lexis-Nexis has really mishandled what was an excellent product. This is especially true because it is currently rumored that the Billing Matters adjunct product may be discontinuted.

PracticeMaster

A highly rated case management application is PracticeMaster by STI (**www.practicemaster.com**). By now this should come as no surprise, but PracticeMaster comes in two versions, too: Basic Edition and Premium Edition. The PracticeMaster Basic Edition is already included if you have the Tabs3 billing software (see the Billing Software chapter). The Basic Edition is just that—basic. The Premium Edition contains a number of useful features that most attorneys would desire. You can view the comparison chart at **www.practicemaster.com/products/practicemaster/ pm_comparison.html**.

PracticeMaster Basic costs $150 for the first user license and each additional one is $50. PracticeMaster Premium costs $295 for the first user license, and each additional license will set you back another $150.

In addition to the two versions mentioned, STI offers PracticeMaster in client server versions, which scales to larger implementations. The Basic client server edition costs $500 for the first user license and $185 for each additional one. The Premium client server edition costs $890 for the first user license and $250 for each additional user. Don't forget to add the cost of the client server environment when calculating the project's total cost. As an example, the STI Server Software is required for any client server implementation of Tabs3 or PracticeMaster. This Server Software could cost from $745 for eight connections up to $5,795 for 1,024 server connections. This product is consistently well-reviewed, but we have seldom seen it implemented in our region.

Finally, it is highly recommended that you obtain the trial version of PracticeMaster. This will help you determine whether the product is right for your practice and installed infrastructure.

Others

There are additional products available, but the vendors aren't public with the cost or system requirements. We are less than impressed with companies that aren't public with their pricing or technical requirements. Products like ProLaw (Thomson Elite) and AbacusLaw (Abacus Data System Incorporated) require you to fill out a contact form so that a representative can contact you about pricing. We're not fond of this practice and recommend a relationship with more open vendors, especially when you're entering this arena and want to make an apples-to-apples comparison.

CHAPTER SIXTEEN

Billing Software

PROBABLY THE SECOND MOST important function of your law practice is billing your clients for services rendered. Practicing law is clearly the most important, but it is nice to actually get paid, thereby ensuring the continued success and sustainability of your practice. Not to mention the practical goals of paying the mortgage and getting the kids through college!

There are a lot of options for generating your bills from a complete manual system to the fully automatic capture and assembly of invoices. There are two components that comprise items in your bills. One is the time component. This component is calculated by taking the hourly rate and applying it to the amount of time spent on a task. You can capture this time manually or automatically while the task is being accomplished. Flat fees are also considered time components, where the dollar amount is applied irrespective of the time spent. The second component is the fixed cost items of the invoice. This would include such expenses as postage, copier costs, filing fees, courier charges, and any other fixed fees. As with the hourly components, you can track these expenses manually or automatically (to some level or another) through the use of technology.

Manual Generation

Pencil and paper are the simplest way to capture time and expense. The manual generation, however, means that you must remember to log your time, number of copies, or whatever other chargeable component needs to be tracked. Make no mistake about it, studies have shown over and over again that this manual tracking results in a lot of lost time and therefore lost dollars. Because a lawyer's time equals money for the most part, many lawyers are shortchanging themselves by not moving to a technology-based solution.

Nevertheless, if this is what you do, on a periodic basis (daily, monthly, the end of the case, and so forth) you total the charges and generate the bill. To save money, many solo practitioners start by using a word processing package to generate their bills. They are professional enough in appearance, but still require manually adding up numbers and multiplying other numbers. There also has to be another method to keep track of payments made by the client and/or transfers of funds from other sources, such as the trust account. As the practice becomes more complicated, the billing process becomes more subject to mistakes.

If you start with a manual method for generating your invoices, try to keep that time as short as possible. Invest in billing software as soon as possible to improve your accuracy, maximize your billable hours, and minimize your losses.

Accounting Software

Some attorneys are actually using a financial accounting package to generate their bills. Probably one of the most popular software applications is QuickBooks by Intuit (**http://quickbooks.intuit.com**). Using QuickBooks to generate invoices allows the firm to have a total financial package, where all sorts of financial reports are available. Another advantage of using QuickBooks is the ability to generate payroll as well. This may not be a compelling reason for many attorneys, especially given the added cost, complexity, and reporting requirements. In general, it's more cost effective to use a service such as ADP or Paychex to handle solo and small firm payrolls. QuickBooks also handles processing of credit card payments, thereby integrating another piece of the financials into a single product.

QuickBooks comes in several different versions and there is even an online version, which allows for access from any computer and does not require any software installation on the computer. We don't recommend using the online version, as it requires that your data be stored at Intuit. Your financial data is highly sensitive, and we recommend that you control your own data and not risk its compromise by holding it at a third party. Consider, too, the possibly severe consequences if the third party is "down" and you can't manage the financial part of your law practice.

Since QuickBooks is an accounting package, some knowledge of financial principles is helpful. For instance, you'll need to set up a chart of accounts for your practice. We recommend consulting with your accountant prior to configuring QuickBooks so that your financial categories are consistent with the accountant's needs.

The QuickBooks versions vary in cost from $99.95 to more than $3,000 for the Enterprise versions. The cost variance is due to the capabilities of the software and the number of concurrent user licenses that are needed. Most solo and small firms will find that QuickBooks Pro is more than sufficient for their needs. The cost is $199.95 for a single user and $549.95 for three users. Accountants love it when attorneys use QuickBooks as their billing software. They can just take the QuickBooks data file at the end of the year and generate tax returns with relative ease.

Billing Specific

Arguably the most popular and widely used billing software in use among solo and small firm attorneys is Timeslips by Sage (**www.timeslips.com**). Timeslips is a billing-specific software package that generates bills, tracks receivables, and manages trust accounting.

Probably one of the reasons for the popularity of Timeslips is that it can be configured specifically for the legal industry. When you first install Timeslips, you select the type of business. This configures Timeslips to use the types of tasks and expenses that are specific to the industry. As an example, when you select the legal profession, default tasks are automatically created that deal with those tasks that are performed in the law office. There will be tasks for consultations, document review, depositions, and so forth. The expenses are also automatically created and would include such costs as copier usage, courier fees, postage, and the like. Trust accounting is also built into Timeslips, which is another reason why the software is very popular in solo and small firm offices.

Timeslips is licensed on a per-machine basis. Each computer that accesses Timeslips will need to purchase a license. In a small office, usually only one computer is used to process billing. The time keepers (typically attorneys) may elect to manually track their time on paper and give the time sheets to the office manager for entry into Timeslips. This arrangement keeps licensing costs down and allows for growth in the law firm. As the firm grows, additional licenses may be purchased and network access configured for the Timeslips database. Those larger firms that may use a terminal server only need licenses for the number of concurrent users. With the expanded interest and implementation of virtual computers, this concurrent license model may be a way to control costs.

Timeslips costs $499.99 for a single station. Additional network stations may be added for $199.99 each. Bundled pricing is also available if you need five or more licenses. Support options are also available for Timeslips. If you have never used Timeslips, it's recommended that a support plan be purchased for the first year of operation. After the first year, we don't recommended prebuying any support unless you intend to use and implement features of the newer versions. Access to the free online knowledge base is usually sufficient to work through most issues that you're likely to experience. You can always purchase support on a per-incident basis if you really get into trouble.

Integrated Packages

Several of the case management products now support integration with billing packages. This means that you enter your information into the case management system and the time is automatically captured for the billing process. There are advantages to using the same vendor for your case management and billing needs. The products are designed to work together and share information in a very efficient manner. However, selecting these "all in one" packages will not give you the best features of each package. If you really want a "best of breed" implementation, then make sure you investigate how the case management and billing packages share the data. Many case management applications provide "links" to billing packages by other vendors. Be careful to understand how to configure these links, especially if it is a manual process. We've seen clients that added tasks to their case management software and forgot to define the linkage to their billing software. This means that you may not bill for the effort when you use these newly defined taks.

LexisNexis has several billing options to address the needs of the solo and small firm law offices. A very popular package is PCLaw (**http://law.lexis nexis.com/back-office-pclaw**) called Lexis Back Office powered by PCLaw. Like other vendors, PCLaw is available in two versions. The version most popular among solo and small firm attorneys is the base product, which is limited to nine timekeepers. If you need more than nine, you will have to purchase PCLaw Pro. The base version of PCLaw is $612.50 for the first user and includes the first year of support. It's $400 for the first user if you don't want to purchase support. Each additional user is $338.25 with support and $300.00 without. The starting cost of the PCLaw Pro version is $4,000 for the first 10 users without support and $4,850 with support for one year. The cost is $400 (without support) for each additional user beyond the initial 10. If you want one-year support, then the cost is $485 per user over 10. Just like the caveats with case management packages, don't forget to add the cost of SQL server if you need to purchase the Pro version. Users are generally quite happy with PCLaw.

Billing Matters is another billing option offered by LexisNexis and is the companion product for the Time Matters case management product. Billing Matters (**http://law.lexisnexis.com/billing-matters**) comes in two versions. The Professional version is fine for solo and small firm offices. The Enterprise version requires a computer with Microsoft SQL and is intended for larger firm environments. The Professional version is $350 for the first user. Additional licenses are $200 per user. The cost per user is lower if you add Billing Matters to a Time Matters installation. We wish to caution readers that may be considering a Billing Matters installation. We believe that LexisNexis will drop support and the availability of Billing Matters in the coming months. Several of our colleagues have the same feeling. Therefore, we would recommend that you investigate PCLaw as your billing component for your Time Matters installation or consider integrated packages from other vendors.

Another popular billing package is Tabs3 by STI. Tabs3 is the companion product to PracticeMaster, which is the case management software from STI. Tabs3 pricing is based on the number of billable entities. Single user prices start at $295 for two timekeepers and go to $1,995 for up to 39 timekeepers. Multiuser network versions start at $495 for two timekeepers up to $3,995 for 39 timekeepers. STI defines a timekeeper as someone whose time is tracked in the software. You can see more information about Tabs3 at **www.practicemaster.com/products/tabs3/tabs3.html**.

A less widely used billing option is provided by Amicus Attorney. A lot of solo and small firms use Amicus Attorney as a practice management package, but few use the billing option. The billing package is called Amicus Accounting 2008 and is available from Gavel & Gown Software (**www.amicusattorney.com/products/prod_overview-accounting.html**). The initial license cost is $349 and each additional license of Amicus Accounting is $249, which makes it one of the lowest cost billing packages. Amicus Accounting can be used as a stand-alone package or in conjunction with the Amicus Attorney software to provide an integrated solution. Several clients have experienced problems with the Amicus accounting package, including such issues as duplicate entries and improper math.

One of the higher level (expensive) billing alternatives is provided by Pro-Law, which is a Thomson Elite product. ProLaw is an integrated package and the billing component is not available as a separate function. Very few solos and small law firms have chosen this route in our experience.

Most of our clients have chosen QuickBooks or Timeslips as a billing package, and they are generally quite happy with what they have chosen—though everything has a learning curve. All of these vendors are happy to let you sample their product in one manner or another, so don't hesitate to try before you buy. Also, if you aren't keen on accounting, talk to your friends who are equally number-challenged and see what has worked for them. In many cases, the choice has been made by someone at the firm who is going to perform the accounting/bookkeeping functions, and that's fine. As long as you stay with one of the "majors," you won't be left scrambling to find someone who knows your obscure time and billing package if that person leaves.

CHAPTER SEVENTEEN

Document Management

DOCUMENT-MANAGEMENT SOFTWARE SOLUTIONS are fairly expensive for the solo or small firm operation. They tend to be used more for enterprise size companies because of their cost and complexity. As the industry matures, vendors are merging the functions of document management, content management, and knowledge management. This is especially true as electronic files are becoming a critical component of discovery. You may see applications described as document-management systems, content management systems, knowledge management systems, or even enterprise content management systems (ECM). Just because a vendor chooses to describe its product in a particular way doesn't mean there is anything unique or special about it. In general, all of the terms previously mentioned are used for applications that organize information. End of story.

The purpose of a document-management system is to organize information into a useable and searchable form. How many times have you looked for a file or document but couldn't remember the name or location? A document-management system allows for fast and easy access to the data, whether in paper or electronic form.

We will mention just a few of the products that are available, but understand that document-management systems are not generally designed for small-scale operations. Xerox's (**http://docushare.xerox.com/index.html**) DocuShare has been around for many years. Just to give you an idea of cost, the entry level DocuShare 6.0 system with 20 seats starts at $4,500, and a 100-seat system of DocuShare CPX 6.0 starts at $45,000. The cost per user will go down as the amount increases, but you can see that this product is intended for larger firms, since there are minimum seat purchase requirements and the overall cost is high for solo and small firm installations.

Interwoven (**www.interwoven.com**) is another product used by law offices to manage documents. Like DocuShare, expect to pay thousands of dollars for this system. It is a highly regarded document-management environment, but is also geared more toward the intermediate to large-scale firms.

Arguably, the most popular and most used document-management system for solos and small firm operations is WORLDOX (**www.worldox.com**). WORLDOX is licensed on a concurrent user basis and not per seat. The cost is around $400 per concurrent user, which makes it very affordable for the solo and small firm, especially since there are no minimum seat-purchase requirements. The application is very robust and easy to use, hence its popularity among the legal community.

Case management systems (see the Case Management chapter) are also used to provide a certain level of document management. Your electronic files are referenced to a client or client matter, making them easily accessible at the click of a mouse. A key point to remember about true document management applications is their stringent enforcement of the classification rules. The user must use the document mangagement system within the configured rules, which sometimes frustrates people because of the rigid requirements. In contrast, using methods that are not specifically document management software aren't restrictive or mandatory. The danger is that data may be "lost" or misfiled when the rules are not stringently enforced.

Many solo and small firm offices are equipped with Adobe's Acrobat product. The later versions of Acrobat provide the ability to manage documents. The collaboration components within Acrobat are used to organize and reference files in a similar way as other document-management systems.

Web-based document-management systems are becoming very popular. The cost per user is typically more than if you purchased the product for use within your firm, but you save on the hardware and internal support costs. The vendor provides the back-end hardware and software for the management of your documents. The nice part about Web-based document-management systems is that the information is accessible from any computer with an Internet connection. The bad part? The vendor is holding your data (which may be highly sensitive client information) and you are subject to the Internet connection's reliability. If you elect to use one of the online document-management systems, be aware of the security precautions for client data being held by a third party. At a minimum, make sure that the connection for accessing the documents is encrypted and that the data is stored in an encrypted form on the provider's equipment.

Finally, a very simple form of document management for solo and small firms is to follow a standard folder and file naming convention along with search software (see the Utilities chapter). Besides the cost for search software, this is a very low-cost solution. Typically, folders are named on a per-client or client-matter basis. Files are then named with a very descriptive name such as <client name> followed by the file purpose, and sometimes the date. As an example, "Rothburg request for admissions.doc" would be the file name for your request for admissions in the Rothburg matter. This is a very manageable method to organize data. As your practice grows, search software may be needed to assist in finding particular files pertaining to specific issues.

Search software such as dtSearch or X1 (see the Utilities chapter) can be used to index the files within your client folders so that you can quickly find the document pertaining to the request for electronic evidence on a partner's Motorola cell phone or some other specific document.

If you are considering the purchase of a document-management system, WORLDOX is an excellent first choice. No matter what product you're considering, see whether there's a trial version available or at least participate in a demo of the product to determine if it meets your firm's needs.

CHAPTER EIGHTEEN

Document Assembly

ESSENTIALLY, DOCUMENT ASSEMBLY SOFTWARE automates the creation of legal documents that are used repeatedly. This would include such documents as wills, leases, contracts, and letters. You can think of document assembly as templates that can be used over and over. This shortens the time for document preparation and increases the efficiency of your practice.

Document assembly software can be specialized for a particular industry or can be of the generic variety. As an example, specialized document assembly software is typically used in estate planning and tax preparation. In those situations, the user answers questions in a survey type of form and the required documents are generated using the answers provided. If you've ever used one of the personal income tax programs (e.g., TurboTax or TaxCut), you've seen how document assembly works.

In law firms, the top three document assembly packages are HotDocs, AIA Contract Documents, and ProDoc. HotDocs (**www.hotdocs.com**) is the most popular document assembly software by a large margin. Hot-Docs is a LexisNexis product and comes in several "flavors." The Standard Edition enables you to turn your word processor documents into interactive and automated templates. You create a template and determine what text to include or exclude, depending upon the user's answers. This is that survey type entry that was described earlier. The presentation walks you through the questions in order to gather the data needed to generate the document. A single copy of HotDocs Standard costs $300.

HotDocs Professional has the same features as the Standard version as well as additional capabilities. The Pro version allows you to create a graphics-based form template as well as allowing the user to change the template view. There is much more flexibility in dealing with variables as part of the assembly logic. Additional automation tools are also available. These are just a few of the additional capabilities with the Professional version. The cost for these added features raises the license cost to $600 per user.

New to the HotDocs product family is the HotDocs 2008 PDF Advantage. PDF Advantage turns PDF documents (e.g., loan applications, IRS forms, court documents, etc.) into an automated HotDocs template. The PDF Advantage option is an add-on to your current HotDocs product. The PDF Advantage Standard offers HotDocs Standard Edition users the convenience of PDF-based HotDocs templates. The cost is $60 per license. The Professional version of PDF Advantage is $100 per license. PDF Advantage Professional allows you to create PDF forms from HotDocs, whereas this feature is not available in the Standard version.

As with a large amount of application software these days, HotDocs is available in a browser version, too. The product is called HotDocs Server Edition and allows for document assembly using a standard Web browser. This is particularly helpful for remote users. Pricing information is available from LexisNexis.

AIA Contract Documents (**www.aia.org/docs_default**) is a specialty package used for design and construction projects, so it's an excellent product for those dealing with construction law. In fact, the product was developed specifically with the law in mind. The generated documents conform to the laws in effect at the time of creation. Also, the AIA documents are intended for nationwide use and are not restricted to specific states. A new, single-seat license that allows for unlimited documents is $979. An unlimited five-seat license is $3,219 and unlimited 10 users is $5,959.

ProDoc (**www.prodoc.com**) is another document assembly application. One of the interesting features of ProDoc is how the licensing works. ProDoc is licensed on a subscription basis. The basic subscription license allows for usage on three computers or three concurrent users. If you install ProDoc on a network, the licensing enforces the three-concurrent-user limit. You can only install ProDoc on three computers if they are stand-alone and not running in a network installation. If you need additional licenses, the cost is $10 per month.

The ProDoc forms are state-specific and currently only available for California, Florida, Texas, and Texas eFiling. The pricing for ProDoc is no longer available online. You must now contact ProDoc, Inc. directly to order the product. There are different document assembly systems available for the supported states. Be sure to check the Web site to see what modules are contained in each package and to verify that your particular practice area is covered.

HotDocs is the clear recommendation for solo and small firm attorneys wanting to embark on document assembly. As a generic package, it is very well-suited for any type of law practice. There are many choices for technical support to include the online knowledge database, discussion lists, and user groups. Many consultants are also well-versed in HotDocs and can provide individual service if needed.

CHAPTER NINETEEN

Collaboration

COLLABORATION MAY NOT BE at the top of your list, especially if you are a solo attorney. However, we're sure that you will have occasion to deal with other attorneys or even have a need to collaborate with your clients on a case. There are some great technology solutions to allow for collaboration—and the kinds of solutions are multiplying week by week. These are just a few of the tools that are available for sharing information and working in a collabrative mode. Calendar sharing is starting to become popular, not so much for the law firm, but for online access by family members.

Social networking is another collaboration area that is gaining in popularity. This seems to be a current trend; however, we haven't yet seen much business value in using the various social networking sites. There's a lot of hype, so one of the authors has patiently put herself out there and made extensive contacts, but thus far she reports that she's been "poked," had sheep thrown at her and received largely self-interested invitations to join webinars and other groups. She remains unimpressed, but continues to watch this phenomenon with interest to see if this volatile new world becomes a real business tool.

Google Docs & Spreadsheets

Probably one of the most well-known of the collaboration tools is Google Docs & Spreadsheets. The popularity of this Web 2.0 application is only surpassed by its great price—free! The application allows you to work on a document or spreadsheet with others and see the modifications in real time. You just use the Web browser on your computer with your Internet connection.

You do need to have a Google identification to use Google Docs & Spreadsheets. Just go to **http://docs.google.com** and enter your logon information. You can also create an account from the main entry page. Besides creating your files from scratch, Google Docs & Spreadsheets allows you to upload files that you've already created on your computer. As an example, you can upload popular file formats like HTML, DOC, XLS, ODT, ODS, RTF, CSV, PPT, SXW, TXT, and so forth, and begin working with them online. You can also e-mail documents to a specific e-mail address that Google creates for you. If you select the upload icon, there are instructions for starting documents via the e-mail function. The interesting thing is that the e-mail address uses the **writely.com** domain, which was the original product name prior to Writely being acquired by Google. Once you've created or uploaded the file to Google, you send an invitation (via e-mail) to those that need to collaborate on the file(s). Edits are viewed in real time. Changes are tracked by each user so you can see who did what to the file. After your file is completed, you can download it to your computer in several supported file formats. The export formats are DOC, XLS, CSV, Open Office, PDF, RTF, and HTML (zipped).

As a practical point, multiple people can collaborate on a file and not everyone needs the same software or version. You can go online and create a file to start the process. Once completed, perhaps you download the file as a DOC file since you use Word as your word processor. Another person downloads the RTF version that they read into an old version of WordPerfect and a third person downloads the ODT version because they use Open Office. Each person downloads the same information, but in a different file format to match what they use on their computer.

The caution with Google Docs & Spreadsheets is that the data is being held by a third party. Obviously, you would not want to use this solution to work on highly proprietary information such as a patent application. Even though you can control file access, Google still holds the "keys" to all of the data.

Acrobat

Today, more and more attorneys have Acrobat (**www.adobe.com/products/acrobat/**), especially if they do e-filing of court documents. Acrobat allows for collaboration with PDF documents so you can conduct shared document reviews that allow the participants to view one another's comments. All three Acrobat versions (Standard, Pro, and Pro Extended) allow for this type of collaboration. Acrobat 9.0 Standard is currently $299, Pro is $449, and Pro Extended is $699. Acrobat Pro Extended has the complete features of Acrobat 9 plus Adobe Presenter and Adobe LiveCycle Designer. These added products allow a great variety of multimedia content to be included in a single PDF file. Attorneys should opt for the Pro version, primarily for the enhanced security and redaction ability. Acrobat Pro 9.0 allows you to create a document that your clients may find useful. It allows Adobe Reader (the free reader version) users to participate in reviews with complete commenting and markup tools, including sticky notes, highlighter, lines, shapes, and stamps. This means that your clients (or other attorneys for that matter) don't have to purchase Acrobat in order to collaborate with you. This feature is not available with Acrobat Standard, hence the recommendation to purchase the Pro version. Consider purchasing Acrobat 8.0 Professional, especially if you can find it at a much reduced cost, since it is one version back. Version 9.0 is the current version, but there aren't any significant enhancements for the legal profession over those legal specific functions that are included in Acrobat 8.0 Professional.

Microsoft Word

Another collaboration tool is the "track changes" feature of Microsoft Word. With this tool, you can see the modifications of each user as they modify the document. The caveat is that the software must be configured to properly identify the user. Some preloaded Office installations have the user configured as something generic like "Owner" or "Satisfied Customer" and not the user's name. You can see how your Office (2003 and prior) installation is configured by going to "Tools, Options" and selecting the "User Information" tab. Word 2007 users would click the Office button in the upper left, select the "word options" button at the bottom and see the user information in the "Popular" menu choice. Once this option is properly configured, the user information will show properly with the track changes. The user also has the ability to insert comments in addition to actually modifying the document contents. As a precaution, do not strip the metadata (as you might normally do for confidentiality reasons) from the document if you are sending it to another party for collaboration. Removing the metadata also removes the tracked changes so the recipient will not see the intended modifications. When you've got the document ready and want to send it to a client, then scrub the metadata!

SharePoint

As time moves on, so does Microsoft's reach into the computing environment. SharePoint is Microsoft's solution for collaboration. Basically, SharePoint is a Web-based server environment that allows the end-user to collaborate on data that is managed through a SharePoint server. There is no special software needed because access is accomplished via a browser.

The cost of SharePoint is considered to be expensive for most solo and small firm operations, especially for new installations. Besides the cost of the server hardware, you will need the server software and CALs. It's going to cost you around $1,000 just for the server software and five CALs, which is the smallest configuration available. However, SharePoint is a free download if you already have Server 2000, 2003, or SBS.

Microsoft is pushing SharePoint in a hard way. It is thought that the current Public Folders function of Exchange will go away in future versions so that you are forced to go with a SharePoint installation to get the same features as you currently get today with a base Exchange installation.

SharePoint is still the rage at legal technology conferences and vendors are promising the world. Will SharePoint live up to all the hype? We've yet to see, but we're watching a lot of early adopters. Of all of Microsoft's major innovations, this may be one that really takes off.

For much more on collaboration tools from two of the greatest experts in the country—Dennis Kennedy and Tom Mighell—see their new book, *The Lawyer's Guide to Collaboration Tools and Technologies* (ABA Law Practice Management Section, 2008), available at the ABA's Web store.

CHAPTER TWENTY

Unified Messaging

WHAT EXACTLY IS UNIFIED messaging and why are so many lawyers excited about it? Overwhelmingly, the primary reason is because they can now get voicemail on their cell phones. Generically, unified messaging is the delivery of traditional voice communications into your e-mail box. This would include the delivery of facsimile transmissions as well. Unified messaging systems began to appear around 2001 and were fairly unsuccessful for the first couple of years. Now they are stable and actually work. This means that there is now (potentially) one location for you to monitor your communications.

The simplest way to implement unified messaging is to have it integrated with your phone system. Some small firms may not even have a phone system and we'll address that issue in a moment. Many of the newer PBX (Private Branch Exchange) systems are incorporating a voicemail card directly into the telephone system chassis. Stand-alone voicemail systems are also an alternative for larger office environments.

For budget purposes, plan on spending around $3,000 or more for a voicemail system with unified messaging. As is true for most technology solutions, your mileage may vary. There are a lot of different ways that vendors implement unified messaging. Some are better than others, and, frankly, some are nothing more than kludge workarounds to make their systems sound more robust than they really are.

There are companies that resell unified messaging solutions, thereby saving you the investment in hardware and software. These solutions are typically available for a monthly fee and you may have to commit to a multi-year contract to obtain the service. Also, you are "stuck" with whatever features and methods the vendor provides. As an example, you may not like the file format for a fax delivery into your in-box, but you'll have to accept what they give you. Another concern is that all of your communications will be going through a third party. This means that your phone calls actually route through their system before being delivered to your location. In that way, they can "capture" a voicemail message or fax and repackage it for delivery to your e-mail address. We are generally not fans of having client data move through third-party providers and would recommend that you first investigate "owned" systems that you can control. While a price tag of $3,000 isn't cheap, the value is so great that a good number of solos and small firms have made the leap and the numbers grow monthly.

We'll attempt to cover some of the concerns and questions you should have when considering to implement a unified messaging solution. These issues are related to equipment that is provided as part of your telephone communication system. The first issue is, What communications are handled by the system? Can it do voice messages and fax transmissions, or just one of them? Even though most systems will handle both voicemail and facsimile transmissions, most firms only use the voice capability and route the faxes to a dedicated fax machine or printer rather than delivery to a specific person's in-box.

So how do you want the voice messages delivered? Most firms will elect to only send an e-mail notification that a voicemail message has been received. This configuration saves bandwidth because the message itself is not transmitted to the e-mail client and stays on the voicemail server. This means that you have to retrieve the message from the voicemail system and is hardly convenient if you're traveling. In fact, some telephone systems are configured to not allow remote connections, even for voicemail retrieval, as a security measure. There are a lot of lawyers that use Black-Berry devices. A large number of them cannot play sound files (especially older models), so sending the message to your phone is pointless. The newer BlackBerry models can play audio files. Make sure that your cell phone can play back the file format for your voicemail if you elect to deliver the message to your in-box.

The other alternative is to deliver the actual message to your in-box. Obviously, this uses a lot more bandwidth, especially if you are delivering it to a cell phone that also receives your e-mail. You'd better have an unlimited data plan for your cell phone if you elect this configuration. Another question for your PBX provider is how they handle the message delivery itself. Is it forwarded to your in-box and then deleted from voicemail? That means there is only one copy of it and you'll never know you received a message if it gets trapped or trashed by your spam filter. If the original stays on the voicemail system and a copy gets delivered to your in-box, does the message light stay lit on your phone? You may not want this, but you may want a visual indication that a voice message was delivered, too.

How does the vendor identify the voice message in your in-box? Is the "From: address" something that is as easily recognizable as the phone system, or does it come from yourself? What does the subject line contain? It is particularly helpful if the caller ID shows in the subject line, but not all vendors package the messages that way. How is the voice message delivered to your e-mail system? Do you have to have a user ID and password configured on your voicemail box that is consistent with your network credentials? If so, you have the issue of constantly synchronizing your logon credentials with the telephone system. Many phone systems only accept numbers as a password so you can't even use letters (forget capitals). This restriction may render your integration unacceptable.

Finally, how do you retrieve your messages? Are they delivered as a standard audio attachment to an e-mail message? This is certainly preferred, since you don't need any special software to listen to the message. Some of the lower cost (and kludge) solutions require that you install a software add-on to your e-mail client to listen to the voice message. This solution won't work if you're trying to deliver the voicemail to your cell phone or if you access your e-mail via a browser. Another problem deals with specific software versions. We had one client that was upgrading to Office 2003, which was not supported by the unified messaging vendor. It was more than eight months before the vendor provided an updated version of the unified messaging client that would work with the 2003 version of Outlook. They are now understandably "gun shy" about upgrading to Office 2007 because of the potential impact on the unified messaging client. As you can see, having specialized software is not a recommended solution. Better to have the voice message packaged as a standard (not proprietary) audio file attachment. That way you can even retrieve your voicemail using a Web browser from an Internet café while on vacation in Rio.

If all of this has given you a headache, don't worry. Make sure your IT consultant reads this chapter and can answer all the questions for you. But make no mistake about it—no one who has successfully implemented unified messaging has ever discarded it. The value of unified messaging is phenomenal—being able to access your voicemail on your cell phone is a remarkable enhancement. You need never worry again about being out of touch. If you prefer not to give clients your home or cell phone number, you'll still get the client's messages. We cannot count the number of times that having voicemail sent to our cell phones has been worth its weight in diamonds.

CHAPTER TWENTY-ONE

Paperless or Paper LESS: The Quest to Sanely Manage Paper in Practice

by Ross L. Kodner, Esq.

WHO ISN'T INTERESTED IN reducing the amount of clutter in their office? Make finding, filing, and sharing files easier by going "paper LESS" rather than "PAPERLESS." Scanning paper documents as searchable PDFs and using a legal document management system to build and manage complete, contiguous electronic client matter files.

> *Water, water, everywhere,*
> *Nor any drop to drink.*
>
> Samuel Taylor Coleridge
> "The Rime of the Ancient Mariner"

> *Paper, paper everywhere,*
> *Nor any page to find.*
>
> Ross L. Kodner
> Thoughts on the Paper LESS Office

Note: I work as an independent technology consultant for law firms. As part of this work, my firm acts as a reseller for certain technology products. However, just as the authors have stated in the preface that the book contains their objective advice, I have strived to provide unbiased advice and product recommendations in this chapter.

LAWYERS AND THEIR STAFFS universally have one thing in common: they are buried in an unending stream of paper that chokes and clogs the flow of work in both private and public law practices. Sometimes getting client work out is more an issue of managing mounds of paper than of applying legal brilliance. Have you ever considered how much time that otherwise would be billable is wasted every day as lawyers and legal staff look for information that can be found only in paper files? There may be hope in getting out from under all that paper.

For years, lawyers have been on a quest for the paperless office, but this concept is likely the greatest lie of the technology age. Our offices never will be paperless, at least in the foreseeable future. We need to accept the fact that even if we reduce the amount of paper we generate, other people will continue to send us paper. Early technology scanning was touted as the great answer, but it is not.

Law Practice in the Age of Instancy

Lawyers and legal professionals in all walks of practice—from SmallLaw to BigLaw, in corporate and government practice—all face the reality of this "Age of Instancy" in which we practice and live. Think of it this way. Twenty-five years ago, do you remember how extraordinary it seemed when the company then known as Federal Express promised that it could deliver a hard copy document, anywhere in the world, by 10:30 AM the next morning? It seemed positively miraculous, didn't it? Today, 10:30 AM the *next* morning seems like an eternity to have to wait; how our perceptions of time and expectations of access to documents and other information have changed.

Today, while on the phone with a client across the continent, if the need to share a document arises, what do we do? Instinctively and without need for any taxing conscious thought, we say, "No problem, I'll e-mail them while we're talking." A five-megabyte collection of attachments zips across the ether and arrives in the client's e-mail in-box, almost before we can finish the sentence. Collaboration, orally, digitally, all happening virtually at the speed of light.

This instant access to information changes our expectations. Clients are "trained" to expect instantaneous everything. Instant access to documents, electronically delivered. Instant responses to questions they pose to their lawyers—such as for when was that deposition scheduled? Or, how much do I have left on my retainer balance? Or, do you have the contact info for that financial forensic consultant you mentioned last week? Law practices that are not able to instantly respond to such "in conversation" queries quickly become labeled as "technopeasants." Effectively, such lawyers can be instantly branded by their clients as being both mechanically and substantively incompetent and frankly, more of an irritant than a professional counselor to the client.

While the "Age of Instancy" may not be a positive development of the human experience, it is what it is: a fact of professional life. Woe unto the lawyer who fails to acknowledge this issue by putting themselves in their clients' shoes and understanding how true it is that the client's perception is the only reality that counts. So what does this have to do with managing paper in our practices? Simply . . . everything.

Paper—Endless Frustration and Expense

Paper is the bane of every law practice's existence. This is actually nothing new—it is one of the endlessly frustrating Great Truths of Law Practice. Paper wastes our time. Paper costs us money. Paper files get lost. Paper hides itself at the most inopportune time. Paper costs money to store. Paper costs yet more money to retrieve. Paper used injudiciously negatively impacts the environment. Paper tends to get coffee or lunch spilled on it in direct proportion to the importance and irreplaceability of the document. In fact, there is a great corollary of life in law practice that says "the more urgently one needs a paper client file, the less likely it is where it is supposed to be."

The Cost of Being Paper-Centric

Think about this question: how much time do you or your staff waste in an average workday, either, (a) looking for paper client files, or (b) looking for information you can only find in paper files? How many of you waste 15 minutes chasing paper? 30 minutes? An hour or more? How many of you have experienced days where the paper file never turns up at all? Or even worse, a staffer starts an expedition to seek out a missing, yet urgently needed paper file. After 15 minutes and no success, the lawyer then chases the staffer who in turn is still chasing the file. So it ends up being 30 staff minutes and 15 lawyer minutes—a phenomenal waste of otherwise billable and productive time.

We can perform some quick legal business math to calculate the value of these endless paper chases. Presume a net realized billed rate of $200/hour—a likely average for solo and small firm lawyers in private practice.

Then presume a billable value of $60/hour for legal assistants or parale-gals. Assume three lawyers wasting an average of 15 minutes per day chasing paper, one legal assistant and one paralegal wasting 30 minutes each day (more for staff because they are often chasing paper on behalf of requesting lawyers). That common small-firm scenario represents a total daily value of otherwise billable/productive time wasted of:

> $150 per day for the lawyers
>
> $60 per day for the staff

That translates to:

> $750 per week for the lawyers, $3000 per month, $36,000 per year
>
> $300 per week for the staff, $1200 per month, $14,400 per year

That represents more than $50,000 in otherwise billable/productive time for this firm. And make no mistake; the effect of $50,000 in revenue never coming back to this firm has precisely the same effect as writing out a $50,000+ check at the end of the year. A basic business operations lesson shows that a reduction of top-line gross revenue has precisely the same negative impact on bottom-line profit as writing a check for $50,000. A cardinal principle of business operations is that a firm does not actually have to generate a check to spend money. Money not coming in has the same effect as that check that draws down from a bank account.

That is the cost of being paper-centric. A $50,000+ hit for a three-lawyer practice. Hardly inconsequential—in fact, a staggering drain of a law prac-tice's only available "product inventory," its billable and productive time.

So with so much at stake in managing the paper chase, why have we heard nothing but stories about failed attempts to go "paperless"? Whether a law practice down the street or more often than not, some government agency that devoured millions of taxpayer dollars in a fruit-less, multi-year paperless office project: failure or at best, a mediocre outcome. Why is this the case? The reason is simple—no matter how much your practice or your company tries to reduce the paper it uses and generates, the rest of the "paper clueless" world (especially budget-challenged government agencies) will inundate you with paper. The reality is clear—paper will be with us for some time to come, perhaps forever. Even if you had to look at this cynically and say that there are too many companies whose livelihoods are derived from paper in some way (e.g., paper companies, copier companies, printer companies, print-ing consumable companies, etc.), you would come to this frustrating and inevitable solution. So is it hopeless? Are we doomed to be perpetual slaves to the printed page?

What if you never had to chase paper files around the office? What if you could find a way to have to touch the paper files less often, or virtually never at all? What if you could "buy back" that wasted 15, 30, 60 or more minutes per day looking for paper necessary for you to serve the needs of clients? What might that mean economically? Even if you took an especially conservative posture in terms of how you viewed the conversation of "wasted paper chasing" time into billable time and cut the above recovery calculation by 50 percent, that would still represent $25,000 per year in "found money," and that's not pocket change for a three-lawyer practice annually.

And what if the answer to this problem cost less than $10,000 in out of pocket costs for software, hardware, and consultative guidance? (approximately $3,000 for software, $3,000 for desktop scanners, approximately $4,000 for planning, process-streamlining, installation and training).

In that 50 percent discounted conservative analysis, the first year net yield is at least $15,000 ($25,000 in converted/recovered billable/productive time less $10,000 in out-of-pocket costs), and then at least $25,000 per year thereafter. A conservative five-year billable/productive net revenue increase of approximately $115,000 in exchange for an approximately $10,000 front-end investment. Wouldn't it be ironic to find out that the best investment you could ever make in your life turned out to be investing in your own law practice? This is the proverbial economic "no-brainer."

Another factor, while more subjective in measurement, but equally tangible in perceived value, is the positive effect on everyone's psyche—on everyone's mental well-being. The endless daily paper chases take a toll psychologically on lawyer and staffer. It is just plain stressful when a paper file eludes location and wastes time, usually at the most inopportune moment. The toll of stress, frustration and angst that missing paper files inflict on legal professionals may be difficult to quantify. But it is nevertheless as real as the fact that the sun rises in the east. Stress lessens our effectiveness; stress drives away valuable employees; stress affects our well-being, especially when we take it home and inflict our work frustrations on our families. And frankly, modern law practice is complicated enough, and aggravating enough so that anything we do that can positively impact our stress levels, while simultaneously filling our firm coffers is something we need to run to, as fast as we can.

Fragment Client Files Defy Common Sense

Being paper-centric in practice brings another inherent anti-common sense inefficiency. One of the core problems in working on client files is that they are always split into two locations. The documents we create are located internally on our PC systems. The client documents we receive from outside sources are stored in our paper filing systems. So, if you want to view all the correspondence on a client's file, you have to look in two separate places—on-screen for your own documents and then you need to track down the paper file and rifle through it to view the externally generated letters. That is, of course, if no one happened to have that particular file in their briefcase at home. Who hasn't experienced the fallout from this irrational and illogical artificial fragmentation of our case files?

Stop the Madness: Become Paper LESS in Your Practice

Fine. You're still reading and slowly becoming a believer in some kind of Paper LESS Office. One where you can avoid wasting time in the paper chase that has haunted you for your entire law practice career. The next question is how does your practice become Paper LESS? Surprisingly easily. With a combination of scanning tools, the wonders of the universally accessible and compatible PDF file format, sound but simple procedures and then some kind of document/e-mail management system, a law practice can undergo a Paper LESS transformation literally overnight. Let's see how . . .

How many of you have had bad scanning experiences over the years? Many of you, in all likelihood . . . and there's a logical reason for all the scanning frustrations of the past. Since the dawn of document scanning, the term "scanning" has been synonymous with "OCR" (optical character recognition). In other words, most people equated scanning with trying to use software to identify the characters on a page and turn the page into an editable word processing document. It was a good idea conceptually, but in practice, even with the best OCR technology available, the process is still far from perfect. For example, with 97 percent OCR accuracy, three incorrect characters out of every 100 could mean as many as 66 errors per page on average. And what if any one of those errors is critical and not detected?

And then, even with the latest greatest OCR software, running on new PCs literally dripping with computing horsepower and fast new scanners . . . the process is about as slow as watching water boil . . . or paint dry . . . or grass growing. How can that be? It's 2009 after all, not 1988. The reason is that when trying to turn scanned pieces of paper into a Word or WordPerfect document, while it has become almost trivial to recognize the raw text on the scanned paper, it is still very difficult to replicate the layout by applying codes, styles, and other formatting tools to produce a usable word processing document. And it is often surprisingly slow— turning that shiny new 40-papers-per-minute scanner, effectively, into a five-pages-per-minute unit. Go ahead and let out that primal scream— we have all been there and we have all similarly suffered.

So stop the madness; the bottom line is that modern scanning should not be equated with OCR. Instead, scanning should be looked at much more simply, as a way, first and foremost, to turn physical into electronic paper. Effectively to photocopy the documents, but not in the traditional way that copying produces a duplicate piece of paper. Rather instead, to photocopy the document to the computer screen—producing a precise duplicate of the scanned paper. And then store it as a searchable (or as Adobe calls it, an "accessible") PDF file. Then use a document management system and well-thought-out document storage procedures with a smart file-naming convention to store the "electronic paper" in your electronic client file cabinet.

And if the on-screen document looks precisely the same as the original piece of paper, why would you ever waste time trying to locate the paper itself? Of course, you wouldn't. You would use your document management system to rapidly navigate through your electronic file cabinet, or use instant search technology to pinpoint the document and pull it up on-screen. No more "Keystone Cops" episodes of staff chasing paper, lawyer chasing staffer. No more drain of otherwise billable or productive time. Instead of those endlessly amusing games of "who the heck has the Jones file," just click, click and you're working: billing time, making more money, *sans* all the paper-chase-related stress that previously dominated your days.

Getting Specific About Being Paper LESS

That's the essence of the Paper LESS Office process. Now let's get specific. What tools do we need? What processes make sense? How do we get from a Paper MORE Office to the Paper LESS Office?

PAPER LESS SIDE BENEFIT: And when you close a Paper LESS file, it's already "electronic paper": You can store it in a convenient byte-sized package (sorry, pun intended). This is a far better alternative for closed file storage than the costly space-hungry storage requirements for physical paper files—which usually end up commandeering an area the size of a starter home.

With a concept that I developed first in 1995 and have since called the "Paper LESS Office," scanning is viewed as a way to turn physical paper into digital paper.[1] When documents are scanned as *images*, the process can be as much as 20 times faster than the processing-intensive and error-ridden OCR approach. On screen, imaged documents that have been scanned as searchable PDFs look precisely like the originals.[2] Even handwriting, preprinted lines, and boxes scan perfectly.

Attorney and litigator Dale Cottam, a partner with the firm of Hirst & Applegate in Cheyenne, Wyoming, explains how his firm uses the Paper LESS Office process:

"When staff and attorneys receive paper documents in the mail, they scan each one using a low cost and efficient Fujitsu ScanSnap S500 scanner (a model since replaced by the new S510 which includes Adobe Acrobat 8.0 Standard), which essentially is a 'PDF machine.' Every person at the firm—staff and attorneys—has a ScanSnap on his or her desk to make converting paper documents to electronic documents second nature.

"Once scanned, the electronic documents are saved in the universally readable PDF format. With a click of the mouse and a few seconds-per-page processing time, the text in the electronic document is converted to searchable text. The original paper document is placed in an expandable file folder and, in most cases, never is touched again. In some instances, the original is mailed to the client.

"The electronic documents are stored in the attorney's electronic in-box using the Worldox document management system,[3] or they are routed directly to the attorney via e-mail. Either way, a copy of the electronic document is saved on the firm's network server, which is backed up nightly.

"Attorneys read the electronic documents on their computer monitors. If they are on the road, they can access the electronic documents through the firm's VPN (virtual private network), a high-speed remote connection."

---

[1] I first put forth my Paper LESS Office concept in an article of the same name in the now defunct *Law Office Computing* magazine in September 1995.

[2] This is a core part of the Paper LESS Office concept, wherein scanned documents stored as PDFs look precisely like the originals, but have searchable and even editable textual content.

[3] Worldox is a product of World Software Inc., one of the three leading legal-focused document/e-mail management and work product retrieval systems, in addition to Interwoven (Interwoven, Inc., formerly known as iManage), and eDOCS (Open Text Corporation, formerly known as PC DOCS Open).

Scanning Systems—What Works?

In terms of scanners, a critical success element is the use of a combination of a centralized, higher-speed scanner or multi-function copier with scanning abilities as well as distributed, decentralized individual desktop scanners. Why both? Why not just rely on that newly leased, monolithic, all-powerful, hulking multi-function copier/printer/scanner down the hall? After all, you're paying for it every month, and it's a wonderfully rapid, high-capacity scanner.

Here is why relying solely on that über-capable multi-function unit will ultimately cause your Paper LESS Office initiative to fail. Let's assume that you have a wire basket next to your super-duper multi-function device down the hall. Everyone puts their documents to be scanned in the basket. Then every Tuesday and Thursday afternoon, your partner's 16-year-old daughter's boyfriend's cousin, 15-year-old "Nick" comes in to scan your documents. Now think about scenario for a moment. How would Nick, the high school scanning clerk have any clue about where to store the documents or what to call them. Because after all, you didn't have the time to paper-clip a note to the document indicating the precise client and matter to store the documents under and an equally precise, descriptive file name. So the odds are, in spite of Nick's best efforts, you'll end up with a jumbled mess.

Instead, the approach that has proven itself in the field over many years places individual desktop direct-to-PDF scanners at, often, *each* PC in the office—lawyers and staff alike. The idea is that inbound paper is distributed to the people who are familiar with the documents and who are familiar with the cases they belong to. These people know where to store the documents; these people know what to call the documents—because these are the cases they actually work on! Lawyers and staff will likely scan different types of documents. Lawyers may scan a few business cards collected at the local lunchtime Rotary Club meeting—all representing prospective clients and possible referral sources. The same lawyer might scan a pertinent article from the latest issue of the *ABA Journal* or their local state bar magazine. Staff is likely to scan case-related documents: incoming correspondence, pleadings received in the mail, etc.

With each person doing their own case-related scanning, the overall scanning burden is distributed and it is accomplished contemporaneously. This yields electronic case files that are made whole in real-time or near real-time. This further means that any lawyer or staff looking at the electronic file onscreen can count on the file being current and being complete. This encourages further reliance on the electronic file by maximizing trust in the new approach.

Of course, when a larger volume of paper comes in, such as several banker's boxes in response to a discovery request, no one will want to scan 10,000 pages at their 20-pages-per-minute desktop scanner with the 25-sheet paper feeder. That is when the staffer trots down the hall and scans using that monster multi-function machine, equipped with a high-capacity paper feeder and blistering 60-pages-per-minute scanning speed. But in this case, the key is that the person scanning is the staffer who is actually familiar with the case and where to store and how to name the electronic paper.

This is an approach that has proven itself—the combination of centralized and decentralized scanning resources. Throw into the mix using the right lawyer or staff resource to scan the documents—the people who best know their own files and their own documents. This works. One approach to the exclusive of the other has inevitably failed in firms that tried just the centralized approach alone.

In terms of USB port-connected desktop scanners, there are a variety of capable products. A consistent favorite over the last several years has been the ScanSnap series from Fujitsu—a well-respected and entrenched producer of scanning systems. With 18-pages-per-minute scanning speed and duplex capability (scans both sides in a single pass), this color-capable printer includes a 25-page feeder with an adjustable guide that can handle stock as small as a business card. The attraction of the ScanSnap series has been a combination of reliability, incredible ease of use via the famous "big green button," the inclusion of a full copy of Adobe Acrobat Standard edition, and reasonable price—street priced in the $400 range with an ever-present $50-per-unit rebate.

Other capable desktop scanners include models from Visioneer, Xerox with its fast 50-pages-per-minute Documate series and Hewlett-Packard, with its venerable ScanJet product line.

PAPER LESS QUICK TIP: a common misconception is that if one scans at a higher resolution, the text recognition results will improve. In fact, often the opposite is true. Lower scanner resolution settings can yield better recognition. At higher resolutions, modern scanners have such capable optics that they can actually become "confused" by the fibers of the papers, which are incorrectly interpreted as characters. Set the resolution to 150-300 dpi for better text recognition results whether using OCR software or producing "searchable" PDF files.

Document Management Systems: The Electronic Glue Holding it Together

The critical element in the Paper LESS Office process is the use of document management technology. Effectively, whether a dedicated, legal-focused document management software application or document management capability intrinsic in a number of practice management software systems, this is the "digital glue" that holds the Paper LESS Office together.

There are four legal document management systems (or perhaps five?) available as of this writing:

♦ Worldox GX from World Software (**www.worldox.com**, available since the late 1980s after starting its life as a DOS application called "Extend-a-File"). While suitable for large firms and deployed in a number of BigLaw organizations, Worldox has traditionally dominated the small and mid-sized law practice marketplace. This has largely been the result of several factors, including: lower cost to acquire and implement because it doesn't require a costly underlying SQL Server database infrastructure, and relative simplicity to implement and to maintain versus its BigLaw-oriented rivals. It integrates tightly with Microsoft Outlook for e-mail management and to many practice management systems including Amicus Attorney (**www.amicusattorney.com**), PracticeMaster (**www.tabs3.com**) and LexisNexis TimeMatters and Total Practice Advantage (**www.timematters.com**).

♦ Interwoven, formerly known as iManage (**www.interwoven.com**), traditionally a larger-firm oriented document management system that relies on a SQL Server database. This more expensive and more complex infrastructure makes this an impractical choice for SmallLaw.

♦ eDocs from OpenText (formerly known as Hummingbird Docs) (**www.opentext.com**): Very similar to the Interwoven system as a BigLaw-oriented, SQL Server-based application. It's quite prevalent in large firms and virtually never seen in small firms.

♦ NetDocuments from Lexis-Nexis (**www.netdocuments.com**). A SaaS product (Software as a Service—in other words, an application that runs in a Web browser with documents either stored on a third-party hosted storage system or on the firm's own Web-accessible servers). SaaS brings its own range of questions and holds promise, but this product is not oriented to smaller firms in terms of pricing or its relatively inability to directly integrate with SmallLaw practice management systems directly.

The Worldox GX (**www.worldox.com**) document management system, the most suitable of the above-listed applications for SmallLaw, organizes paper documents received in the mail and scanned as searchable PDFs; e-mails received with attachments (when used with Microsoft Outlook, an e-mail even with multiple attachments can be organized by Worldox in one step, rather than the usual daunting series of multiple save steps otherwise required); and documents created within the office, regardless of which software program was used to create them (for example, Word, Word Perfect, Excel, Adobe Acrobat/PDFs, digital photos, voice-mail files, etc.). The same Worldox interface is common to all file-saving processes, simplifying the approach and cutting the learning curve. Effectively, your electronic filing system can be set up and organized to precisely parallel your file cabinet/red-rope brown expandable file/manila folder-based paper system, making it easy for anyone to understand, regardless of whether they are a legal techno-pro or a techno-peasant.

Most practice management software, programs such as Amicus Attorney, PracticeMaster, ProLaw, TimeMatters and others, incorporate some degree of document and e-mail management as well. Or, in the alternative, leading practice management systems typically integrate with leading legal document management systems. Which approach is best? The internalized document management functionality of a practice management application of the third-party, separate but integrated dedicated document manager? The answers are specific to the unique document management approaches of each practice management system. But the bottom line for most firms is that the more robust features and the mandatory, must-save-it-the-document-management's-way approach of third party tools tends to prevail. Often built-in document management segments of practice management systems do not require that every document be saved to client case files. Experience shows that the failure to make this an automatically mandatory process results in people lazily taking shortcuts, and creating incomplete case files that cannot be relied on.

In essence, the document management system takes the scanned document-turned PDF and organizes it in this manner:

When one clicks the File Save, or File Save As functions in Acrobat, instead of the software's native file-management dialogue boxes appearing, the Worldox document management system pops up.

To save the file, one selects which "File Cabinet" (or in Worldox-speak, the "profile group")—examples commonly include Client Documents, Forms & Templates, Firm Administration, and Personal Files.

Then one is presented with a "Profile" screen that allows the user, instead of having to navigate through an often mystifying and inconsistent Windows folder tree, a set of fill-in-the-blanks for information such as the Client Name, the Matter Name, the type of document (e.g., correspondence, contracts, pleadings, etc.), who authored the document, and sometimes the historical date of the document or a notation as to whether the document has been reviewed by a responsible party in the firm). These pieces of information are accessible very rapidly from quick-pick lists or even in a single-click approach that calls up a template called a "Quick Profile" for oft-accessed client matters or subject files. All in all, much more concise and faster than common Windows navigation.

Fill in a plain-English name for the document, ideally following a logical file-naming convention agreed upon and consistently used by everyone in the file and click "ok." The scanned electronic paper is now organized and connected to the same, cohesive, contiguous and complete electronic matter file as are all the internally generated word processing files, spreadsheets, presentations, digital photos, downloaded PDFs and e-mails with their attachments—a complete electronic case file.

Later, documents can be found by simply "checking the electronic file cabinet"—clicking to the Client, the Matter and then an electronic version of the manila folder. If it is not possible or efficient to locate the desired document by viewing the electronic file cabinet and then scanning the list of plain-English filenames, the document can nearly instantly be found by searching for key text within the document itself using a word or phrase search similar to a query in Google, Lexis, or Westlaw. Worldox searches are infinitely faster than the brain-dead "File, Find" function in the Windows XP operating system and every bit as fast as the modern desktop search products such as Windows Desktop Search, Copernic, X1 and Google Desktop.

Even a scanned document, which is otherwise just an "image" like a digital photo, can be located using key terms, provided that when it was scanned the image was converted to searchable text using Adobe Acrobat (version 7 and up, Standard or Professional edition, or an equivalent product that does automated batch conversions of scanned "image" PDFs into "searchable" PDFs such as AquaForest's Autobahn DX (**www.aquaforest.com**), which can be set to find all new "image" PDFs stored during the day and convert them in an automated fashion into "searchable" PDFs v. the cumbersome, more manual/attended process using Adobe Acrobat itself—which can otherwise slow the scanning process considerably).

The Real-World: Comments from the Trenches in the Paper Wars

From his perspective as a busy commercial litigator, Dale Cottam further observes that "in today's fast-paced technology world, many clients expect their attorneys to be at least at the same technical level of capability and proficiency as they are. With the relatively low cost of available scanning hardware and document management software, firms can keep up with their clients. Part of the cost of this technology will be offset by decreased expenses for postage and long-distance phone calls associated with faxing and increases in productivity. The level of stress involved in searching for lost files and documents is reduced dramatically."

Figure 1 demonstrates the real-world and practical advantages of electronic versus paper files. If you're considering moving from paper to electronic files, but aren't sure how to start, here are a few suggestions:

FIGURE 1   Advantages of Electronic versus Paper Files

Factor	Paper Files	Electronic Files
Active Case and Archival Storage	Paper is expensive to file, route, and store.	Electronic documents are cheap and convenient to store. If paper files are shredded after closure of a case, physical storage costs are cut dramatically, yet lawyers have all old file information accessible instantly via electronic searches. Archiving on the firm's server(s) takes the place of physical storage. Electronic paper can always be reduced to physical paper if ever needed.
Finding Lost Documents	Finding lost documents takes significant time, sometimes many hours, including relying on discussion with other lawyers and staff. If a document has been misfiled, it may never be found.	Searching for electronic documents is nearly instantaneous using a search engine contained within document management systems. A lawyer who previously wasted 15 minutes per day looking for paper files can easily recover valuable billable time by immediately locating "electronic paper" and not chasing paper files around the office.
		If these 15 minutes can be converted into billable time v. wasted non-billable time, the financial effect can be an additional $12,000 per year for a lawyer who bills an average of $200/hour.

FIGURE 1   Advantages of Electronic versus Paper Files—*(Continued)*

Factor	Paper Files	Electronic Files
File Sharing	Collaborating on paper documents is cumbersome. Copies must be made and routed at significant cost in terms of staff time and consumables, not to mention the negative environment impact.	Collaboration, revisions, remote access, and sharing of important information are very convenient when documents are stored electronically.
Remote Access	Paper documents must be mailed or faxed off site. Or lawyers needing to work on files need to remember to bring boxes of paper with them.	Electronic documents are available to attorneys and staff over secure remote connections or can be received via e-mail—in effect instantaneously accessing every single document on single matter without regard to the location of the physical paper file.
Protecting Client Files from Disaster	Irreplaceable paper documents are at risk for being destroyed by fire and natural disasters.	Electronic files are easily backed up and stored off-site and can be restored to the firm's network in little time. As "electronic paper," this is the first realistic way to protect paper files from damage by fire and natural disasters.
Brief Banking	Tedious filing and organization must be used to quickly find relevant briefs in paper format; most firms fail to keep it updated so few people would ever trust it.	Electronic versions of briefs and memos can be located quickly using search engines and indexers that look for specific words or phrases. Finally, the mythical "brief bank" becomes usable, current and reliable.
E-mail Management	To make a "complete" paper file you would need to print every e-mail and attachment that is sent and received. Sheer inefficient insanity.	The Paper LESS Office approach using the Worldox (or other) document management system allows you to save (via "profiling") a stand-alone e-mail or one with multiple attachments in a single step, for both inbound and outbound messages. This results in a nearly miraculous answer to a spiraling issue of e-mail chaos that plagues so many law practices today. E-mails are merely correspondence—and they belong connected to the complete electronic case file—as opposed to being eternally buried in the bottomless hole that is the in-box of most people.

Make the commitment to the process of moving toward the Paper LESS goal. Give up on the pipe dream of being paperless—it's simply not realistic and will lead to inevitable disappointment—you're not going to rid your practice entirely of paper. The key is dedication, an emphasis on standardized and consistent procedures, as well as a commitment to educating your team of people about the "why's" and not merely the "how's" for making the shift to viewing electronic matter files as the primary, "sacred" and complete client file.

Ensure your hardware is up to the demands of the increased amount of scanning, processing, and storage. This would be the ideal time to send your six-year-old PC stations to a virtual "assisted living center" and replace them with a set of contemporary desktop and laptop systems. Dual monitors (or even three displays) are very helpful for simultaneously scanning, storing, and viewing multiple programs being worked on—with a practice management system, your word processor(s), Acrobat, Outlook or another e-mailer, a time entry input application, and one or more Web browsers—the productivity payoff is normally instantaneous. Network servers need the ability to store one to five gigabytes per attorney per year. Having a reliable, multiple level backup system and testing it often with "mini test restores" is critical, as are all the normal recommended elements of a sound data backup process.

Plan and test. Spending time planning as well as the "pilot" testing of systems and procedures avoiding fits and starts before the Paper LESS concept rolled out firm wide.

The Paper LESS Bottom Line . . .

A truly paperless office is never going to happen while any of us are alive. No matter how diligently you try to reduce or even eliminate the paper you generate, other people will send you paper for years to come. However, a Paper LESS Office is rapidly and practically attainable. You can use less paper, have to find less paper and touch paper less often, thereby becoming significantly more efficient in your practice. By employing a creative and commonsense approach to scanning, turning physical paper into searchable electronic paper, and by leveraging anti-paper PDF tools, you can transform your desktop landscape and find more profits, more enjoyment, and better client responsiveness in your practice.

Ross L. Kodner, an attorney, is president and founder of MicroLaw Inc., an international legal technology and law practice management consultancy based in Milwaukee and founded in 1985 at the dawn of the legal PC age. For nearly a quarter century he has been the principal of Micro-

Law, Inc., serving private law firms, corporate and government legal departments worldwide. A former long-time member of the ABA TECHSHOW planning board, he also served four years as Chair of the ABA Law Practice Management Section's Computer and Technology Division. Currently he is an ABA General Practice, Solo and Small Firm Division active member and both founded and served as Co-Chair of the Division's National Solo and Small Firm Conference, as well as founding and serving as first Chair of the Wisconsin Solo and Small Firm Conference. He is also a prolific author and Continuing Legal Education (CLE) speaker, with over 400 published articles and more than 1,300 CLE sessions since the 1980's. As long as he can remember, his mottos have been "Friends don't let friends word process without Reveal Codes (even with Word)!" and Red Adair's famous statement that "if you think hiring an expert is expensive, try hiring an amateur." He can be reached via **rkodner@microlaw.com**, **www.microlaw.com** and **www.rossipsa.com**.

CHAPTER TWENTY-TWO

Tomorrow in Legal Tech

"Then I will try to make the best guess I can."
Mr. Spock in *Star Trek IV: The Voyage Home* (1986)

When it comes to the predicting the future of legal tech, we can do no better than Mr. Spock. You just can't keep up with legal technology. Here we were, all set to predict that Microsoft would be forced to extend the life of Windows XP and, wouldn't you know it, it was just announced that Microsoft has decided to do exactly that. After saying that it was going to stop supplying all XP media after January 31, 2009, Microsoft has bowed to external pressure and extended that date through July 31, 2009.

The business world has largely decided to skip Vista entirely, so our next prediction is that many folks will simply wait for Windows 7 and hope that there is no repeat of the Vista debacle.

Last year, we talked about the "Scotty, beam me up" fantasy becoming more and more real. It certainly has turned out that way for us. As of this year, our GPS devices not only talk to us, we can talk to them. Likewise, we can place a phone call by voice command in our cars. And it really works—the voice recognition technology is superb. We have become Scotty, and we are content!

Though the iPhone continues to be the toy of choice for many lawyers, and has become more business-friendly over the course of the year, it still does not have the full functionality of our Windows-based Treos. We're not changing; we're not about to lose functionality to be part of the "in crowd" with the trendy iPhone on a crummy network. We have to say that the allure of the iPhone probably won't fade, but the attraction of the Windows-based cell phones may increase as lawyers come to better understand the price/benefits comparison. As for the BlackBerry, the outages this year have removed some of the BlackBerry's luster. Windows-based cell phones are still BlackBerry killers in our judgment.

Will Google become a true contender to Microsoft? Google has made some interesting moves recently, yielding to European pressure and reducing the amount of time it hangs on to identifiable data from 18 months to six. It unleashed its own browser, Chrome, which had an inauspicious beginning as it was released with some serious vulnerabilities. Can Chrome compete? Hard to imagine shaking Internet Explorer loose from its grip on the general public, but Google has been a surprise victor before.

It's the economy, stupid. That old political slogan sure as heck applies to the coming year. Economic uncertainty is bound to mean that law firms will become more budget-conscious, deliberating longer over software and hardware purchases, more keenly studying the best bang for the buck. As always when the economy has a cold, training programs are likely to get the flu. People will spend as little as possible on training in the coming months, irrespective of its value. IT support? Expect to see a lot of changes as law firms seek less expensive IT support. Our prediction is that this will lead to a lot of bad decisions, as the best legal tech firms are not cheap, but can solve problems more quickly—and avoid them by being proactive. The lowest hourly cost doesn't necessarily translate to a smaller bill.

Handling legal IT has become, and will continue to be, more challenging as law firms increasingly have a distributed environment. There are so many more peripheral and mobile devices to account for in a law firm—it is no wonder that data management is so complex.

Collaboration among lawyers is moving along, but more slowly than we would have thought. That slowness may be accentuated by a poor economy, but as collaboration bring efficiencies with it, perhaps it won't dawdle as much as we fear. The ABA recently published a guide to lawyer collaboration, *The Lawyer's Guide to Collaboration Tools and Technologies*, by noted legal technologists Tom Mighell and Dennis Kennedy. It is an excellent beginning for those exploring how to collaborate and leverage the power of collaboration for their law practice. We are seeing the use of SharePoint trickling down from the NLJ 250 to other firms, so there is hope!

Likewise, Web 2.0 applications have continued to emerge, but they don't seem to have a clear sense of themselves yet. Though they are capable of much, they haven't figured out what's practical. They are looking for a payoff that they haven't yet found. That will change over time, but how much time is something of a mystery. One exception would be Google's success with their productivity products. Google has indicated that several major corporations will be using their online word processor, spreadsheet and other Web 2.0 applications rather than the traditional Microsoft suites.

Social networking exploded this year, more's the pity. Dutifully, one of the authors has put herself out there—everywhere—and accepted everyone's invitation to be a friend. So far, she's been poked, had sheep thrown at her, had folks ask for jobs or referrals (like she needs more of that), received political solicitations, and garnered invites to book and movie clubs as well as free webinars from vendors. Her conclusion? *This stuff is one giant "time-suck."* She will continue to monitor this phenomenon because it has obvious possibilities if anyone actually figures out how to use these sites for a practical purpose. She glumly predicts she'll have another 1,000 "friends" next year with no better sense of what to do with this medium than they displayed this year.

The legal world has embraced "green" in a big way, and that, we predict, will continue. There was some sort of critical mass realized this year in the legal profession. You'd be hard pressed to find a large law firm that doesn't want to boast of its new, greener image. The American Bar Association spends a lot of time on this issue, and lawyers are listening. "Green" seminars are packed as lawyers want to impact their environment and make a sustainable law practice.

Virtualization is one of the technologies that is helping to facilitate this greener footprint. We predict an increase in server virtualization even down to the solo and small firm environments. This is no longer a technology for the large firms. Small firms are seeing the benefit of virtualization, especially as they impelement more robust case management solutions.

Judges continue to get smarter about courtroom technology and especially about electronic discovery. A raft of decisions this year awarding sanctions certainly suggests that any lawyer who doesn't know her way around ESI (electronically stored information) will want to bone up and soon. It's pretty easy to see that judges are continuing to work hard to come up to speed on all things e-discovery related and that this trend is likely to continue.

The blogosphere continues to expand—the one shift we've seen, that we expect to continue, is that there are "rock stars" among the bloggers, those who have consistently turned out high-quality work with a great deal of valuable content. Podcasting, as we predicted last year, has grown relatively slowly by comparison. We're not expecting a rapid expansion there.

A trend we noted last year, the shift from paper advertising to online advertising, continues at the same rate. 65 percent of potential clients begin their search for a lawyer online, so it comes as no surprise that lawyers are rethinking (or pitching) their yellow page ads, and pumping more money into their Web sites, online directories, etc.

We've actually seen more of a shift to Macs by solos and small firms than we had anticipated. Those who have "drunk the Kool Aid" have grown exponentially. We are seeing legal conferences include at least one "Mac for Lawyers" session on a regular basis. This remains, and we predict it will remain, primarily a solo/small firm phenomenon.

Electronic data discovery (EDD) firms may have an interesting time, given the economic slowdown (boy, is that a euphemism). The "whales" have huge overheads—can they sustain themselves when corporate clients are busy slashing budgets and bringing EDD in-house? There may be a slaughter at the top, for those who need the $100,000-plus cases to stay in business. Stats have indicated that more than half of the corporations surveyed report that they have settled cases rather than subject themselves to the cost of EDD and the uncertainty of litigation.

Records management has been a force of its own, as corporations strive to get litigation ready. One of the interesting changes we've seen (at Morrison & Foerster), and that we expect to see more of, is having records management systems grab e-mail on the way in or out and have it duplicated and tagged with retention codes. That way, no matter *what* the user does with the e-mail, it really doesn't matter; the system has handled it.

Outsourcing has had an interesting year, with the release of the ABA's opinion on the topic on August 5, 2008. While it "blesses" outsourcing generally, we believe the many requirements attached to outsourcing, particularly foreign outsourcing, may stop solos and small firms in their tracks. Larger firms can perform their due diligence more easily and justify initial expenditures of time and money by the huge cost savings, especially for EDD review. And it is certainly true that cutting costs will mean happier clients—and happier clients are more likely to stick around.

All in all, we ate our hat, nicely seasoned, on a few issues, but last year's predictions held up fairly well. We won't bet the mortgage money on this year's predictions, but we're optimistic that we've identified at least some of the major issues and their probable resolutions. What we do for a living involves, metaphorically, riding a bolt of lightning. It's a joy ride, but there is a lot of peril lurking.

We comfort ourselves with the words of Abraham Lincoln: "The best thing about the future is that it comes only one day at a time."

Glossary*

Active Directory
Active Directory (AD) is an implementation of LDAP directory services by Microsoft for use primarily in Windows environments. Its main purpose is to provide central authentication and authorization services for Windows based computers. Active Directory also allows administrators to assign policies, deploy software, and apply critical updates to an organization. Active Directory stores information and settings in a central database. Active Directory networks can vary from a small installation with a few hundred objects, to a large installation with millions of objects.

ActiveSync
ActiveSync is a synchronization program developed by Microsoft. It allows a mobile device to be synchronized with either a desktop PC, or a server running Microsoft Exchange Server, PostPath Email and Collaboration Server, Kerio MailServer or Z-push.

Adware
Adware is any software package which automatically plays, displays, or downloads advertising material to a computer after the software is installed on it or while the application is being used. Some types of adware are also spyware and can be classified as privacy-invasive software.

AppleCare Protection Plan
Apple's warranty with a new product is 90 days complimentary telephone support and a one-year hardware guarantee. These can both be extended to a three-year (for computers) or two-year (for iPods and iPhones) warranty and telephone support (inclusive of the initial support) through the

---

*This glossary was compiled from definitions available online at Wikipedia (**www.wikipedia.org**).

AppleCare Protection Plan packs, which can be purchased separately within the initial one-year warranty, or simultaneously with new Apple products, mainly Macs, iPods, and iPhones.

ATA/IDE

Advanced Technology Attachment (ATA) is a standard interface for connecting storage devices such as hard disks and CD-ROM drives inside personal computers. The standard is maintained by X3/INCITS committee T13. Many synonyms and near-synonyms for ATA exist, including abbreviations such as IDE and ATAPI.

Auto Document Feeder (ADF)

Auto Document Feeder (ADF) is a feature in multifunction or all-in-one printers, fax machines, photocopiers, and scanners that takes several pages and feeds the paper one page at a time into the scanner, allowing the user to scan (and thereby copy, print, or fax) multiple-page documents without having to manually replace each page.

Boot Camp

Boot Camp is a utility included with Apple Inc.'s Mac OS X v10.5 "Leopard" operating system that assists users in installing Microsoft Windows XP or Windows Vista on Intel-based Macintosh computers. Boot Camp guides users through non-destructive re-partitioning (including resizing of an existing HFS+ partition, if necessary) of their hard disk drive and using the Mac OS X Leopard disc to install Windows drivers. In addition to device drivers for the hardware, the disc includes a control panel applet for selecting the boot operating system while in Windows.

Byte

Byte (pronounced "bite," IPA: /ba_t/) is a unit of measurement of information storage, most often consisting of eight bits. In many computer architectures it is a unit of memory addressing.

Category 5e Cable (Cat5e)

Category 5e Cable (Cat5e) is an enhanced version of Cat 5 that adds specifications for far end crosstalk. It was formally defined in 2001 in the TIA/EIA-568-B standard, which no longer recognizes the original Cat 5 specification. Although 1000BASE-T was designed for use with Cat 5 cable, the tighter specifications associated with Cat 5e cable and connectors make it an excellent choice for use with 1000BASE-T. Despite the stricter performance specifications, Cat 5e cable does not enable longer cable distances for Ethernet networks: cables are still limited to a maximum of 328 ft (100 m) in length (normal practice is to limit fixed ("horizontal") cables to 90 m to allow for up to 5 m of patch cable at each end). Cat 5e cable performance characteristics and test methods are defined in TIA/EIA-568-B.2-2001.

Category 6 Cable (Cat6)
Category 6 Cable (Cat6), commonly referred to as Cat 6, is a cable standard for Gigabit Ethernet and other network protocols that is backward compatible with the Category 5/5e and Category 3 cable standards. Cat-6 features more stringent specifications for crosstalk and system noise. The cable standard provides performance of up to 250 MHz and is suitable for 10BASE-T/100BASE-TX and 1000BASE-T (Gigabit Ethernet). It is expected to suit the 10GBASE-T (10Gigabit Ethernet) standard, although with limitations on length if unshielded Cat 6 cable is used.

Cathode Ray Tube (CRT)
Cathode Ray Tube (CRT) is an evacuated glass envelope containing an electron gun (a source of electrons) and a fluorescent screen, usually with internal or external means to accelerate and deflect the electrons. When electrons strike the fluorescent screen, light is emitted.

CD-ROM
CD-ROM is a Compact Disc that contains data accessible by a computer. While the Compact Disc format was originally designed for music storage and playback, the format was later adapted to hold any form of binary data. CD-ROMs are popularly used to distribute computer software, including games and multimedia applications, though any data can be stored (up to the capacity limit of a disc).

Central Processing Unit (CPU)
Central Processing Unit (CPU) or sometimes just processor, is a description of a certain class of logic machines that can execute computer programs. This broad definition can easily be applied to many early computers that existed long before the term "CPU" ever came into widespread usage. However, the term itself and its initialism have been in use in the computer industry at least since the early 1960s (Weik 1961). The form, design, and implementation of CPUs have changed dramatically since the earliest examples, but their fundamental operation has remained much the same.

Client Access License (CALs)

Client Access License (CALs) is a kind of software license, distributed by Microsoft, to allow clients to connect to its server software programs.

Code Division Multiple Access (CDMA)

Code Division Multiple Access (CDMA) employs spread-spectrum technology and a special coding scheme (where each transmitter is assigned a code). In communications technology, there are only three domains that can allow multiplexing to be implemented for more efficient use of the available channel bandwidth and these domains are known as time, frequency and space. CDMA divides the access in signal space.

Computer Monitor

Computer Monitor is a piece of electrical equipment which displays viewable images generated by a computer without producing a permanent record. The word "monitor" is used in other contexts; in particular in television broadcasting, where a television picture is displayed to a high standard. A computer display device is usually either a cathode ray tube or some form of flat panel such as a TFT LCD. The monitor comprises the display device, circuitry to generate a picture from electronic signals sent by the computer, and an enclosure or case. Within the computer, either as an integral part or a plugged-in interface, there is circuitry to convert internal data to a format compatible with a monitor.

Computer Virus

Computer Virus is a computer program that can copy itself and infect a computer without permission or knowledge of the user. However, the term "virus" is commonly used, albeit erroneously, to refer to many different types of malware programs. The original virus may modify the copies, or the copies may modify themselves, as occurs in a metamorphic virus. A virus can only spread from one computer to another when its host is taken to the uninfected computer, for instance by a user sending it over a network or the Internet, or by carrying it on a removable medium such as a floppy disk, CD, or USB drive. Additionally, viruses can spread to other computers by infecting files on a network file system or a file system that is accessed by another computer.

Contrast Ratio

Contrast Ratio is a measure of a display system, defined as the ratio of the luminosity of the brightest color (white) to that of the darkest color (black) that the system is capable of producing. A high contrast ratio is a desired aspect of any display, but with the various methods of measurement for a system or its part, remarkably different measured values can sometimes produce similar results.

DAT72 Backup Tapes

DAT72 stores up to 36 GB uncompressed (72 GB compressed) on a 170 meter cartridge. The DAT 72 standard was developed by HP and Certance. It has the same form-factor and is backwards compatible with DDS-3 and -4.

Database Application

A computer database is a structured collection of records or data that is stored in a computer system. A database usually contains software so that a person or program can use it to answer queries or extract desired information. The term "database" refers to the collection of related records, and the software should be referred to as the database management system (DBMS).

DDR2 SDRAM

DDR2 SDRAM double-data-rate two synchronous dynamic random access memory is a random access memory technology used for high speed storage of the working data of a computer or other digital electronic device.

Digital Copiers

In recent years, all new photocopiers have adopted digital technology, replacing the older analog technology. With digital copying, the copier effectively consists of an integrated scanner and laser printer. This design has several advantages, such as automatic image quality enhancement and the ability to "build jobs" or scan page images independently of the process of printing them. Some digital copiers can function as high-speed scanners; such models typically have the ability to send documents via e-mail or make them available on a local area network.

Digital Subscriber Line (DSL)

Digital Subscriber Line (DSL) is a family of technologies that provide digital data transmission over the wires of a local telephone network.

Digital Visual Interface (DVI)

Digital Visual Interface (DVI) is a video interface standard designed to maximize the visual quality of digital display devices such as flat panel LCD computer displays and digital projectors. It was developed by an industry consortium, the Digital Display Working Group (DDWG). It is designed for carrying uncompressed digital video data to a display.

Display Resolution
The display resolution of a digital television or computer display typically refers to the number of distinct pixels in each dimension that can be displayed. It can be an ambiguous term especially as the displayed resolution is controlled by different factors in cathode ray tube (CRT) and flat panel or projection displays using fixed picture-element (pixel) arrays.

Domain Controller
On Windows Server Systems, the domain controller (DC) is the server that responds to security authentication requests (logging in, checking permissions, etc.) within the Windows Server domain.

Dots Per Inch (dpi)
Dots Per Inch (dpi) is a measure of printing resolution, in particular the number of individual dots of ink a printer or toner can produce within a linear one-inch (2.54 cm) space.

DVD
DVD (also known as "Digital Versatile Disc" or "Digital Video Disc") is a popular optical disc storage media format. Its main uses are video and data storage. Most DVDs are of the same dimensions as compact discs (CDs) but store more than 6 times as much data.

E-mail Spam
E-mail Spam is the practice of sending unwanted e-mail messages, frequently with commercial content, in large quantities to an indiscriminate set of recipients.

Encryption/Decryption
Encryption/Decryption is the process of transforming information (referred to as plaintext) using an algorithm (called cipher) to make it unreadable to anyone except those possessing special knowledge, usually referred to as a key. The result of the process is encrypted information (in cryptography, referred to as ciphertext). In many contexts, the word encryption also implicitly refers to the reverse process, decryption (e.g. "software for encryption" can typically also perform decryption), to make the encrypted information readable again (i.e., to make it unencrypted).

Enhanced Definition Television (EDTV)
Enhanced-definition television, extended-definition television, or EDTV is a Consumer Electronics Association (CEA) marketing shorthand term for certain digital television (DTV) formats and devices. EDTV generally

refers to video with picture quality beyond what is broadcastable in NTSC or PAL, but not sharp enough to be considered high-definition television (HDTV). A DVD player with progressive output is considered the lower end of this class, when playing a progressively encoded disc. (The maximum EDTV frame rate of 60 per second is not possible from a DVD.) The common implementations of EDTV are 480 or 576-line signals in progressive scan, as opposed to 50-60 interlaced fields per second (see NTSC, or PAL and SECAM). These are commonly referred to as "480p" and "576p" respectively. In comparison, a standard-definition television (SDTV) signal is broadcast with interlaced frames and is commonly referred to as "480i" or "576i." EDTV can also refer to a display device that has a maximum resolution of 480p or 576p.

Extensible Markup Language (XML)

Extensible Markup Language (XML) is a general-purpose markup language. It is classified as an extensible language because it allows its users to define their own elements. Its primary purpose is to facilitate the sharing of structured data across different information systems, particularly via the Internet. It is used both to encode documents and serialize data.

FireWire

FireWire is Apple Inc.'s brand name for the IEEE 1394 interface (although the 1394 standard also defines a backplane interface). It is also known as i.LINK (Sony's name). It is a serial bus interface standard, for high-speed communications and isochronous real-time data transfer, frequently used in a personal computer (and digital audio/digital video).

FireWire 400

FireWire 400 can transfer data between devices at 100, 200, or 400 Mbit/s data rates.

FireWire 800

FireWire 800 (Apple's name for the 9-pin "S800 bilingual" version of the IEEE 1394b standard) was introduced commercially by Apple in 2003. This newer 1394 specification (1394b) and corresponding products allow a transfer rate of 786.432 Mbit/s via a new encoding scheme termed beta mode. It is backwards compatible to the slower rates and 6-pin connectors of FireWire 400. However, while the IEEE 1394a and IEEE 1394b standards are compatible, FireWire 800's connector is different from FireWire 400's connector, making the legacy cables incompatible. A bilingual cable allows the connection of older devices to the newer port.

Gigabyte
A gigabyte (derived from the SI prefix giga-) is a unit of information or computer storage meaning either exactly 1 billion bytes (1000^3, or 10^9) or approximately 1.07 billion bytes (1024^3). It is commonly abbreviated as Gbyte or GB.

Global System for Mobile communications (GSM)
Global System for Mobile communications (GSM) is the most popular standard for mobile phones in the world. Its promoter, the GSM Association, estimates that 82% of the global mobile market uses the standard. GSM is used by over 2 billion people across more than 212 countries and territories. Its ubiquity makes international roaming very common between mobile phone operators, enabling subscribers to use their phones in many parts of the world. GSM differs from its predecessors in that both signaling and speech channels are digital call quality, and so is considered a second generation (2G) mobile phone system. This has also meant that data communication were built into the system using the 3rd Generation Partnership Project (3GPP).

Hard Disk Drive
Hard Disk Drive, commonly referred to as a hard drive, hard disk or fixed disk drive, is a non-volatile storage device which stores digitally encoded data on rapidly rotating platters with magnetic surfaces. Strictly speaking, "drive" refers to a device distinct from its medium, such as a tape drive and its tape, or a floppy disk drive and its floppy disk.

Hash Function
Hash Function is a reproducible method of turning some kind of data into a (relatively) small number that may serve as a digital "fingerprint" of the data. The algorithm "chops and mixes" (i.e., substitutes or transposes) the data to create such fingerprints. The fingerprints are called hash sums, hash values, hash codes, or simply hashes.

High Definition Multimedia Interface (HDMI)
High Definition Multimedia Interface (HDMI) is a licensable compact audio/video connector interface for transmitting uncompressed digital streams.

High Definition TV (HD)
High Definition TV (HD) is a digital television broadcasting system with greater resolution than traditional television systems (NTSC, SECAM, PAL). HDTV is digitally broadcast because digital television (DTV) requires less bandwidth if sufficient video compression is used.

Hub

Hub is a device for connecting multiple twisted pair or fiber optic Ethernet devices together, making them act as a single network segment. Hubs work at the physical layer (layer 1) of the OSI model, and the term layer 1 switch is often used interchangeably with hub. The device is thus a form of multiport repeater. Network hubs are also responsible for forwarding a jam signal to all ports if it detects a collision.

IEEE

The Institute of Electrical and Electronics Engineers or IEEE (read i triple e) is an international non-profit, professional organization for the advancement of technology related to electricity. It has the most members of any technical professional organization in the world, with more than 360,000 members in around 175 countries.

Intel Core 2 Duo Processor

The Core 2 brand refers to a range of Intel's consumer 64-bit dual-core and MCM quad-core CPUs with the x86-64 instruction set, and based on the Intel Core microarchitecture, which derived from the 32-bit dual-core Yonah laptop processor.

Intel Corporation (Intel)

Intel Corporation (Intel) is the world's largest semiconductor company and the inventor of the x86 series of microprocessors, the processors found in most personal computers.

Internet Information Services (IIS)

Internet Information Services (IIS) is a set of Internet-based services for servers using Microsoft Windows. It is the world's second most popular Web server in terms of overall Web sites, behind Apache HTTP Server.

Internet Protocol Address (IP)

An IP address (Internet Protocol address) is a unique address that certain electronic devices currently use in order to identify and communicate with each other on a computer network utilizing the Internet Protocol standard (IP)—in simpler terms, a computer address. Any participating network device—including routers, switches, computers, infrastructure servers (e.g., NTP, DNS, DHCP, SNMP, etc.), printers, Internet fax machines, and some telephones—can have its own address that is unique within the scope of the specific network. Some IP addresses are intended to be unique within the scope of the global Internet, while others need to be unique only within the scope of an enterprise.

Intrusion Detective System (IDS)

Intrusion Detective System (IDS) is a piece of hardware that detects unwanted manipulations of computer systems, mainly through the Internet. The manipulations may take the form of attacks by crackers. An intrusion detection system is used to detect several types of malicious behaviors that can compromise the security and trust of a computer system. This includes network attacks against vulnerable services, data driven attacks on applications, host based attacks such as privilege escalation, unauthorized logins and access to sensitive files, and malware (viruses, trojan horses, and worms).

IPsec (IP Security)

IPsec (IP Security) is a suite of protocols for securing Internet Protocol (IP) communications by authenticating and/or encrypting each IP packet in a data stream.

iSight Camera

iSight Camera is a webcam developed and marketed by Apple Inc. The iSight was sold retail as an external unit which connects to a computer via FireWire cable and comes with a set of mounts to place it atop any current Apple display, laptop computer, or all-in-one desktop computer. The term is also used to refer to the camera built into Apple's iMac, MacBook and MacBook Pro computers.

Keyboard

In computing, a keyboard is a peripheral partially modeled after the typewriter keyboard. Physically, a keyboard is an arrangement of rectangular buttons, or keys. A keyboard typically has characters engraved or printed on the keys; in most cases, each press of a key corresponds to a single written symbol. However, to produce some symbols requires pressing and holding several keys simultaneously or in sequence; other keys do not produce any symbol, but instead affect the operation of the computer or the keyboard itself.

Laser Printer

Laser Printer is a common type of computer printer that rapidly produces high quality text and graphics on plain paper. Like photocopiers, laser printers employ a xerographic printing process but differ from analog photocopiers in that the image is produced by the direct scanning of a laser beam across the printer's photoreceptor.

Light-Emitting Diode (LED)

Light-Emitting Diode (LED) is a semiconductor diode that emits incoherent narrow-spectrum light when electrically biased in the forward direction of the p-n junction, as in the common LED circuit. This effect is a form of electroluminescence.

Linear Tape-Open (LTO or LTO2)

Linear Tape-Open (LTO or LTO2) is a magnetic tape data storage technology developed as an open alternative to the proprietary Digital Linear Tape (DLT). The technology was developed and initiated by Seagate, Hewlett-Packard, and IBM. The standard form-factor of LTO technology goes by the name "Ultrium."

Liquid Crystal Display (LCD)

A liquid crystal display (LCD) is a thin, flat display device made up of any number of color or monochrome pixels arrayed in front of a light source or reflector. It is often utilized in battery-powered electronic devices because it uses very small amounts of electric power.

Macintosh AirPort

AirPort is a local area wireless networking brand from Apple Inc. based on the IEEE 802.11b standard (also known as Wi-Fi) and certified as compatible with other 802.11b devices. A later family of products based on the IEEE 802.11g specification is known as AirPort Extreme. The latest family of products is based on the draft-IEEE 802.11n specification and carries the same name.

Macintosh/Macs

Macintosh, or for newer models, Mac, is a brand name which covers several lines of personal computers designed, developed, and marketed by Apple Inc. The original Macintosh was released on January 24, 1984; it was the first commercially successful personal computer to feature a mouse and a graphical user interface (GUI) rather than a command line interface. Apple consolidated multiple consumer-level desktop models into the 1998 iMac, which sold extremely well. Current Mac systems are mainly targeted at the home, education, and creative professional markets. They are the aforementioned (though upgraded) iMac and the entry-level Mac mini desktop models, the workstation-level Mac Pro tower, the MacBook, MacBook Air and MacBook Pro laptops, and the Xserve server.

MagSafe Power Adapter

MagSafe Power Adapter is a power connector introduced in conjunction with the MacBook Pro at the Macworld Expo in San Francisco on January 10, 2006. The MagSafe connector is held in place magnetically. As a result, if it is tugged on—for instance, by someone tripping over the cord—it comes out of the socket safely, without damaging it or the computer or pulling the computer off its table or desk.

Media Access Control Address (MAC)

Media Access Control Address (MAC) is a quasi-unique identifier attached to most network adapters (NICs). It is a number that acts like a name for a particular network adapter, so, for example, the network cards (or built-in network adapters) in two different computers will have different names, or MAC addresses, as would an Ethernet adapter and a wireless adapter in the same computer, and as would multiple network cards in a router.

Megabyte

A megabyte is a unit of information or computer storage equal to either 10^6 (1,000,000) bytes or 2^{20} (1,048,576) bytes, depending on context. In rare cases, it is used to mean 1000x1024 (1,024,000) bytes. It is commonly abbreviated as Mbyte or MB.

Message-Digest Algorithm 5 (MD5)

Message-Digest Algorithm 5 (MD5) is a widely used cryptographic hash function with a 128-bit hash value. As an Internet standard (RFC 1321), MD5 has been employed in a wide variety of security applications, and is also commonly used to check the integrity of files. An MD5 hash is typically expressed as a 32-character hexadecimal number.

Microsoft Exchange Server

Microsoft Exchange Server is a messaging and collaborative software product developed by Microsoft. It is part of the Microsoft Servers line of server products and is widely used by enterprises using Microsoft infrastructure solutions. Exchange's major features consist of electronic mail, calendaring, contacts and tasks, and support for the mobile and Web-based access to information, as well as supporting data storage.

Microsoft SQL Server

Microsoft SQL Server is a relational database management system (RDBMS) produced by Microsoft. Its primary query language is Transact-SQL, an implementation of the ANSI/ISO standard Structured Query Language (SQL) used by both Microsoft and Sybase.

Microsoft Windows

Microsoft Windows is the name of several families of software operating systems by Microsoft. Microsoft first introduced an operating environment named Windows in November 1985 as an add-on to MS-DOS in response to the growing interest in graphical user interfaces (GUIs). Microsoft Windows eventually came to dominate the world's personal computer market, overtaking Mac OS, which had been introduced previously. At the 2004 IDC Directions conference, IDC Vice President Avneesh Saxena stated that Windows had approximately 90% of the client operating system market. The most recent client version of Windows is Windows Vista. The current server version of Windows is Windows Server 2003. The successor to Windows Server 2003, Windows Server 2008, is currently being beta tested.

Modem

Modem (from modulator-demodulator) is a device that modulates an analog carrier signal to encode digital information, and also demodulates such a carrier signal to decode the transmitted information. The goal is to produce a signal that can be transmitted easily and decoded to reproduce the original digital data.

Mouse

In computing, a mouse (plural mice or mouses) functions as a pointing device by detecting two-dimensional motion relative to its supporting surface. Physically, a mouse consists of a small case, held under one of the user's hands, with one or more buttons. It sometimes features other elements, such as "wheels," which allow the user to perform various system-dependent operations, or extra buttons or features can add more control or dimensional input. The mouse's motion typically translates into the motion of a pointer on a display.

MP3

MPEG-1 Audio Layer 3, more commonly referred to as MP3, is a digital audio encoding format. This encoding format is used to create an MP3 file, a way to store a single segment of audio, commonly a song, so that it can be organized or easily transferred between computers and other devices such as MP3 players.

Network Address Translation (NAT)

Network Address Translation (NAT) is a technique of transceiving network traffic through a router that involves re-writing the source and/or destination IP addresses and usually also the TCP/UDP port numbers of IP packets as they pass through.

Network Card/Adapter

Network adapter, LAN Adapter or NIC (network interface card) is a piece of computer hardware designed to allow computers to communicate over a computer network.

Optical Character Recognition (OCR)

Optical Character Recognition (OCR) usually abbreviated to OCR, is the mechanical or electronic translation of images of handwritten, typewritten or printed text (usually captured by a scanner) into machine-editable text.

Peripheral Devices

In computer hardware, a peripheral device is any device attached to a computer in order to expand its functionality. Some of the more common peripheral devices are printers, scanners, disk drives, tape drives, microphones, speakers, and cameras.

Personal Digital Assistants (PDAs)

Personal Digital Assistants (PDAs) are handheld computers, but have become much more versatile over the years. PDAs are also known as small computers or palmtop computers. PDAs have many uses: calculation, use as a clock and calendar, accessing the Internet, sending and receiving E-mails, video recording, typewriting and word processing, use as an address book, making and writing on spreadsheets, scanning bar codes, use as a radio or stereo, playing computer games, recording survey responses, and Global Positioning System (GPS). Newer PDAs also have both color screens and audio capabilities, enabling them to be used as mobile phones (smartphones), Web browsers, or portable media players. Many PDAs can access the Internet, intranets or extranets via Wi-Fi, or Wireless Wide-Area Networks (WWANs). Many PDAs employ touch screen technology.

Portable Document Format (PDF)

The Portable Document Format (PDF) is the file format created by Adobe Systems in 1993 for document exchange. PDF is fixed-layout document format used for representing two-dimensional documents in a manner independent of the application software, hardware, and operating system.

Private Branch Exchange (PBX)

Private Branch Exchange (PBX) is a telephone exchange that serves a particular business or office, as opposed to one that a common carrier or telephone company operates for many businesses or for the general public.

PS/2 Connector

PS/2 Connector is used for connecting a keyboard and a mouse to a PC-compatible computer system. Its name comes from the IBM Personal System/2 series of personal computers, with which it was introduced in 1987. The PS/2 mouse connector generally replaced the older DE-9 RS-232 "serial mouse" connector, while the keyboard connector replaced the larger 5-pin DIN used in the IBM PC/AT design. The keyboard and mouse interfaces are electrically similar with the main difference being that open collector outputs are required on both ends of the keyboard interface to allow bidirectional communication. If a PS/2 mouse is connected to a PS/2 keyboard port (or if a PS/2 keyboard is connected to a PS/2 mouse port), the mouse (or keyboard) will not be recognized by the computer.

Radio-Frequency Identification (RFID)

Radio-Frequency Identification (RFID) is an automatic identification method, relying on storing and remotely retrieving data using devices called RFID tags or transponders. An RFID tag is an object that can be applied to or incorporated into a product, animal, or person for the purpose of identification using radiowaves. Some tags can be read from several meters away and beyond the line of sight of the reader.

RAID-5

A RAID 5 uses block-level striping with parity data distributed across all member disks. RAID 5 has achieved popularity due to its low cost of redundancy. Generally, RAID 5 is implemented with hardware support for parity calculations. A minimum of 3 disks is generally required for a complete RAID 5 configuration.

Random Access Memory (RAM)

Random Access Memory (RAM) (usually known by its acronym, RAM) is a type of computer data storage. Today it takes the form of integrated circuits that allow the stored data to be accessed in any order, i.e., at random. The word random thus refers to the fact that any piece of data can be returned in a constant time, regardless of its physical location and whether or not it is related to the previous piece of data.

Redundant Arrays of Independent Disks (RAID)

Redundant Arrays of Independent Disks (RAID) is the most common definition of RAID. Other definitions of RAID include "Redundant Arrays of Independent Drives" and "Redundant Arrays of Inexpensive Drives." RAID is an umbrella term for computer data storage schemes that divide and replicate data among multiple hard disk drives. RAID's various designs balance or accentuate two key design goals: increased data reliability and increased I/O (input/output) performance.

Remote Desktop Protocol (RDP)

Remote Desktop Protocol (RDP) is a multi-channel protocol that allows a user to connect to a computer running Microsoft Terminal Services. Clients exist for most versions of Windows (including handheld versions), and other operating systems such as Linux, FreeBSD, Solaris and Mac OS X. The server listens by default on TCP port 3389. Microsoft refers to the official RDP client software as either Remote Desktop Connection (RDC) or Terminal Services Client (TSC).

Revolutions Per Minute (RPM)

Revolutions per minute (abbreviated rpm, RPM, r/min, or r·min^{-1}) is a unit of frequency: the number of full rotations completed in one minute around a fixed axis. It is most commonly used as a measure of rotational speed or angular velocity of some mechanical component.

Rootkits

Rootkits is a program (or combination of several programs) designed to take fundamental control (in Unix terms "root" access, in Windows terms "Administrator" access) of a computer system, without authorization by the system's owners and legitimate managers. Access to the hardware (i.e., the reset switch) is rarely required as a rootkit is intended to seize control of the operating system running on the hardware. Typically, rootkits act to obscure their presence on the system through subversion or evasion of standard operating system security mechanisms. Often, they are also Trojans as well, thus fooling users into believing they are safe to run on their systems. Techniques used to accomplish this can include concealing running processes from monitoring programs, or hiding files or system data from the operating system.

Router

Router is a piece of hardware that connects together two or more different networks (e.g., LAN to WAN) whose job is to route data data between the networks.

Scanning Resolution

Scanning Resolution describes the detail of the scanned image. The term applies equally to digital images, film images, and other types of images. Higher resolution means more image detail.

Secure Sockets Layer (SSL)

Secure Sockets Layer (SSL) is a cryptographic protocol that provides secure communications on the Internet for such things as Web browsing, e-mail, Internet faxing, instant messaging and other data transfers.

Serial Advanced Technology Attachment (SATA)

Serial Advanced Technology Attachment (SATA) is a computer bus primarily designed for transfer of data between a computer and storage devices (like hard disk drives or optical drives). The main benefits are faster transfers, ability to remove or add devices while operating (hot swapping), thinner cables that let air cooling work more efficiently, and more reliable operation with tighter data integrity checks than the older Parallel ATA interface.

Serial Attached SCSI (SAS)

Serial Attached SCSI (SAS) is a computer bus technology primarily designed for transfer of data to and from computer data storage devices such as hard drives, CD-ROM and DVD tape drives, and similar devices. SAS is a serial communication protocol for direct attached storage (DAS) devices. It is designed for the corporate and enterprise market as a replacement for parallel SCSI, allowing for much higher speed data transfers than previously available, and is backwards-compatible with SATA drives.

Server

A server is an application, or device that performs services for connected clients as part of a client-server architecture. A server application, as defined by RFC 2616 (HTTP/1.1), is "an application program that accepts connections in order to service requests by sending back responses." Server computers are devices designed to run such an application or applications, often for extended periods of time with minimal human direction. Examples of d-class servers include Web servers, e-mail servers, and file servers.

Service Set Identifier (SSID)

Service Set Identifier (SSID) is a name used to identify the particular 802.11 wireless LANs to which a user wants to attach. A client device will receive broadcast messages from all access points within range advertising their SSIDs, and can choose one to connect to based on pre-configuration, or by displaying a list of SSIDs in range and asking the user to select one.

SHA Hash Functions

SHA Hash Functions are five cryptographic hash functions designed by the National Security Agency (NSA) and published by the NIST as a U.S.

Federal Information Processing Standard. SHA stands for Secure Hash Algorithm. Hash algorithms compute a fixed-length digital representation (known as a message digest) of an input data sequence (the message) of any length. The five algorithms are denoted SHA-1, SHA-224, SHA-256, SHA-384, and SHA-512. The latter four variants are sometimes collectively referred to as SHA-2. SHA-1 produces a message digest that is 160 bits long; the number in the other four algorithms' names denote the bit length of the digest they produce.

Shadow Copy
Shadow Copy (also called Volume Snapshot Service or VSS) is a feature introduced with Windows Server 2003, and available in all releases of Microsoft Windows thereafter, that allows taking manual or automatic backup copies or snapshots of a file or folder on a specific volume at a specific point in time. It is used by NTBackup and the Volume Shadow Copy service to backup files. In Windows Vista, it is used by Windows Vista's backup utility, System Restore and the Previous Versions feature.

Small Computer System Interface (SCSI)
Small Computer System Interface (SCSI) is a set of standards for physically connecting and transferring data between computers and peripheral devices. The SCSI standards define commands, protocols, and electrical and optical interfaces. SCSI is most commonly used for hard disks and tape drives, but it can connect a wide range of other devices, including scanners and CD drives. The SCSI standard defines command sets for specific peripheral device types; the presence of "unknown" as one of these types means that in theory it can be used as an interface to almost any device, but the standard is highly pragmatic and addressed toward commercial requirements.

Smartphone
Smartphone is a mobile phone offering advanced capabilities beyond a typical mobile phone, often with PC-like functionality.

Spyware
Spyware is computer software that is installed surreptitiously on a personal computer to intercept or take partial control over the user's interaction with the computer, without the user's informed consent. While the term spyware suggests software that secretly monitors the user's behavior, the functions of spyware extend well beyond simple monitoring. Spyware programs can collect various types of personal information, but can also interfere with user control of the computer in other ways, such as

installing additional software, redirecting Web browser activity, accessing Web sites blindly that will cause more harmful viruses, or diverting advertising revenue to a third party. Spyware can even change computer settings, resulting in slow connection speeds, different home pages, and loss of Internet or other programs.

Stereophonic Sound (Stereo)

Stereophonic sound, commonly called stereo, is the reproduction of sound, using two or more independent audio channels, through a symmetrical configuration of loudspeakers, in such a way as to create a pleasant and natural impression of sound heard from various directions, as in natural hearing. It is often contrasted with monophonic (or "monaural," or just mono) sound, where audio is in the form of one channel, often centered in the sound field.

SuperDrive

SuperDrive is a term that has been used by Apple Inc. for two different storage drives: from 1988–1999 to refer to a high-density floppy disk drive capable of reading all major 3.5" disk formats; and from 2001 onwards to refer to a combined CD/DVD reader/writer. Once use of floppy disks started declining, Apple reused the term to refer to the (originally Pioneer-built) DVD writers built into its Macintosh models, which can read and write both DVDs and CDs. As of December 2006, SuperDrives are combination DVD ±R/±RW and CD-R/RW writer drives offering speeds of 4x-36x and supporting the DVD-R, DVD+R, DVD+R DL, DVD±RW, DVD-9, CD-R, and CD-RW formats along with all normal read-only media.

Switch

Switch is a computer networking device that connects network segments. Low-end network switches appear nearly identical to network hubs, but a switch contains more "intelligence" (and comes with a correspondingly slightly higher price tag) than a network hub. Network switches are capable of inspecting data packets as they are received, determining the source and destination device of that packet, and forwarding it appropriately. By delivering each message only to the connected device it was intended for, a network switch conserves network bandwidth and offers generally better performance than a hub.

Tagged Image File Format (TIFF)

Tagged Image File Format (TIFF) is a container format for storing images, including photographs and line art. It is now under the control of Adobe. Originally created by the company Aldus for use with what was then called "desktop publishing." The TIFF format is widely supported by image-manipulation applications, by publishing and page layout applications, by scanning, faxing, word processing, optical character recognition and other applications.

Tape Drive

Tape Drive is a data storage device that reads and writes data stored on a magnetic tape. It is typically used for archival storage of data stored on hard drives. Tape media generally has a favorable unit cost and long archival stability.

Terminal Services

Terminal Services is a component of Microsoft Windows (both server and client versions) that allows a user to access applications and data on a remote computer over any type of network, although normally best used when dealing with either a Wide Area Network (WAN) or Local Area Network (LAN), ease and compatibility with other types of networks may differ and vary. Terminal Services is Microsoft's implementation of thin-client terminal server computing, where Windows applications, or even the entire desktop of the computer running terminal services, are made accessible from a remote client machine.

Time Machine

Time Machine is a backup utility developed by Apple which is included with Mac OS X v10.5.

Universal Serial Bus (USB)

Universal Serial Bus (USB) is a serial bus standard to interface devices. USB was designed to allow peripherals to be connected using a single standardized interface socket and to improve plug-and-play capabilities by allowing devices to be connected and disconnected without rebooting the computer (hot swapping). Other convenient features include providing power to low-consumption devices without the need for an external power supply and allowing many devices to be used without requiring manufacturer specific, individual device drivers to be installed.

UNIX

UNIX is a computer operating system originally developed in 1969 by a group of AT&T employees at Bell Labs including Ken Thompson, Dennis Ritchie and Douglas McIlroy. Today's Unix systems are split into various branches, developed over time by AT&T as well as various commercial vendors and non-profit organizations.

USB Thumb Drive

USB flash drives are NAND-type flash memory data storage devices integrated with a USB (universal serial bus) connector. They are typically small, lightweight, removable and rewritable.

Video Card/Graphics Adapter

Video Card/Graphics Adapter also referred to as a graphics accelerator card, display adapter, graphics card, and numerous other terms, is an item of personal computer hardware whose function is to generate and output images to a display.

Video Graphics Array (VGA)

The term Video Graphics Array (VGA) refers either to an analog computer display standard, the 15-pin D-subminiature VGA connector, first marketed in 1988 by IBM, or the 640x480 resolution itself. While this resolution has been superseded in the computer market, it is becoming a popular resolution on mobile devices.

Virtual Private Network (VPN)

Virtual Private Network (VPN) is a communications network tunneled through another network, and dedicated for a specific network. One common application is secure communications through the public Internet, but a VPN need not have explicit security features, such as authentication or content encryption. VPNs, for example, can be used to separate the traffic of different user communities over an underlying network with strong security features.

Web 2.0

The phrase Web 2.0 is a trend in Web design and development and can refer to a perceived second generation of Web-based communities and hosted services—such as social-networking sites, wikis, and folksonomies—which aim to facilitate creativity, collaboration, and sharing between users. The term gained currency following the first O'Reilly Media Web 2.0 conference in 2004. Although the term suggests a new version of the World Wide Web, it does not refer to an update to any technical specifications, but to changes in the ways software developers and end-users use webs.

Wi-Fi

Wi-Fi is a wireless technology brand owned by the Wi-Fi Alliance intended to improve the interoperability of wireless local area network products based on the IEEE 802.11 standards. Common applications for

Wi-Fi include Internet and VoIP phone access, gaming, and network connectivity for consumer electronics such as televisions, DVD players, and digital cameras.

Wi-Fi Protected Access (WPA)

Wi-Fi Protected Access (WPA) is a class of systems to secure wireless (Wi-Fi) computer networks. It was created in response to several serious weaknesses researchers had found in the previous system, Wired Equivalent Privacy (WEP). WPA implements the majority of the IEEE 802.11i standard, and was intended as an intermediate measure to take the place of WEP while 802.11i was prepared.

Windows Recycle Bin

Windows Recycle Bin is temporary storage for files that have been deleted in a file manager by the user, but not yet permanently erased from the physical media. Typically, a recycle bin is presented as a special file directory to the user (whether or not it is actually a single directory depends on the implementation), allowing the user to browse deleted files, undelete those that were deleted by mistake, or delete them permanently (either one by one, or by the "Empty Trash" function).

Windows SharePoint Services

Windows SharePoint Services or Windows SharePoint is the basic part of SharePoint, offering collaboration and document management functionality by means of Web portals, by providing a centralized repository for shared documents, as well as browser-based management and administration of them. It allows creation of Document libraries, which are collections of files that can be shared for collaborative editing. SharePoint provides access control and revision control for documents in a library.

Wired Equivalent Privacy (WEP)

Wired Equivalent Privacy (WEP) is a deprecated algorithm to secure IEEE 802.11 wireless networks. Wireless networks broadcast messages using radio, so are more susceptible to eavesdropping than wired networks. When introduced in 1999, WEP was intended to provide confidentiality comparable to that of a traditional wired network.

Index

Selected Books from . . .
THE ABA LAW PRACTICE MANAGEMENT SECTION

The Lawyers Guide to Collaboration Tools and Technologies: Smart Ways to Work Together
By Dennis Kennedy and Tom Mighell
This first-of-its-kind guide for the legal profession shows you how to use standard technology you already have and the latest "Web 2.0" resources and other tech tools, like Google Docs, Microsoft Office and Share-Point, and Adobe Acrobat, to work more effectively on projects with colleagues, clients, co-counsel and even opposing counsel. In *The Lawyer's Guide to Collaboration Tools and Technologies: Smart Ways to Work Together*, well-known legal technology authorities Dennis Kennedy and Tom Mighell provides a wealth of information useful to lawyers who are just beginning to try these tools, as well as tips and techniques for those lawyers with intermediate and advanced collaboration experience.

The Lawyer's Guide to Marketing on the Internet, Third Edition
By Gregory H. Siskind, Deborah McMurray, and Richard P. Klau
In today's competitive environment, it is critical to have a comprehensive online marketing strategy that uses all the tools possible to differentiate your firm and gain new clients. The Lawyer's Guide to Marketing on the Internet, in a completely updated and revised third edition, showcases practical online strategies and the latest innovations so that you can immediately participate in decisions about your firm's Web marketing effort. With advice that can be implemented by established and young practices alike, this comprehensive guide will be a crucial component to streamlining your marketing efforts.

The Lawyer's Field Guide to Effective Business Development
By William J. Flannery, Jr.
"In this wonderful book, Bill Flannery, who changed the legal marketplace forever, does what he's been doing so effectively throughout his extraordinary career—he teaches lawyers how to sell. How can you build your firm's business without it?"
—Richard S. Levick, Esq., President and CEO, Levick Strategic Communications

Long-term, profitable client relationships form the foundation for the enduring success of any law firm. Winning and retaining long-term, attractive clients doesn't happen by accident. In his new book, The Lawyer's Field Guide to Effective Business Development, renowned legal marketer Bill Flannery shares his practical approach to acquiring and refining the face-to-face skills necessary for winning and keeping valuable clients.

In a handy, pocket-sized format, this unique guidebook is designed so you can take it with you as you travel in search of new business. The chapters are organized chronologically to take you step by step from your initial search for clients through the process of building and maintaining long-term profitable client relationships.

The Electronic Evidence and Discovery Handbook: Forms, Checklists, and Guidelines
By Sharon D. Nelson, Bruce A. Olson, and John W. Simek
The use of electronic evidence has increased dramatically over the past few years, but many lawyers still struggle with the complexities of electronic discovery. This substantial book provides lawyers with the templates they need to frame their discovery requests and provides helpful advice on what they can subpoena. In addition to the ready-made forms, the authors also supply explanations to bring you up to speed on the electronic discovery field. The accompanying CD-ROM features over 70 forms, including, Motions for Protective Orders, Preservation and Spoliation Documents, Motions to Compel, Electronic Evidence Protocol Agreements, Requests for Production, Internet Services Agreements, and more. Also included is a full electronic evidence case digest with over 300 cases detailed!

The Lawyer's Guide to Extranets: Breaking Down Walls, Building Client Connections
By Douglas Simpson and Mark Tamminga
An extranet can be a powerful tool that allows law firms to exchange information and build relationships with clients. This new book shows you why extranets are the next step in client interaction and communications, and how you can effectively implement an extranet in any type of firm. This book will take you step-by-step through the issues of implementing an extranet, and how to plan and build one. You'll get real-world extranet case studies, and learn from the successes and failures of those who have gone before. Help your firm get ahead of the emerging technologies curve and discover the benefits of adopting this new information tool.

The Law Firm Associate's Guide to Personal Marketing and Selling Skills
By Catherine Alman MacDonagh and Beth Marie Cuzzone
This is the first volume in ABA's new groundbreaking Law Firm Associates Development Series, created to teach important skills that associates and other lawyers need to succeed at their firms, but that they may have not learned in law school. This volume focuses on personal marketing and sales skills. It covers creating a personal marketing plan, finding people within your target market, preparing for client meetings, "asking" for business, realizing marketing opportunities, keeping your clients, staying in touch with your network inside and outside the firm, and more. An accompanying trainer's manual illustrating how to best structure the sessions and use the book is available to firms to facilitate group training sessions.

Many law firms expect their new associates to hit the ground running when they are hired on. Although firms often take the time to bring these associates up to speed on client matters, they can be reluctant to invest the time needed to train them how to improve personal skills such as marketing. This book will serve as a brief, easy-to-digest primer for associates on how to develop and use marketing and selling techniques.

ABA **LAW PRACTICE MANAGEMENT SECTION**
MARKETING • MANAGEMENT • TECHNOLOGY • FINANCE

The Lawyer's Guide to Marketing Your Practice, Second Edition

Edited by James A. Durham and Deborah McMurray

This book is packed with practical ideas, innovative strategies, useful checklists, and sample marketing and action plans to help you implement a successful, multi-faceted, and profit-enhancing marketing plan for your firm. Organized into four sections, this illuminating resource covers: Developing Your Approach; Enhancing Your Image; Implementing Marketing Strategies and Maintaining Your Program. Appendix materials include an instructive primer on market research to inform you on research methodologies that support the marketing of legal services. The accompanying CD-ROM contains a wealth of checklists, plans, and other sample reports, questionnaires, and templates—all designed to make implementing your marketing strategy as easy as possible!

The Lawyer's Guide to Increasing Revenue: Unlocking the Profit Potential in Your Firm

By Arthur G. Greene

Are you ready to look beyond cost-cutting and toward new revenue opportunities? Learn how you can achieve growth using the resources you already have at your firm. Discover the factors that affect your law firm's revenue production, how to evaluate them, and how to take specific action steps designed to increase your returns. You'll learn how to best improve performance and profitability in each of the key areas of your law firm, such as billable hours and rates, client relations and intake, collections and accounts receivable, technology, marketing, and others. Included with the book is a CD-ROM featuring sample policies, worksheets, plans, and documents designed to aid implementation of the ideas presented in the book. Let this resource guide you toward a profitable and sustainable future!

The Lawyer's Guide to Strategic Planning: Defining, Setting, and Achieving Your Firm's Goals

By Thomas C. Grella and Michael L. Hudkins

This practice-building resource is your guide to planning dynamic strategic plans and implementing them at your firm. You'll learn about the actual planning process and how to establish goals in key planning areas such as law firm governance, competition, opening a new office, financial management, technology, marketing and competitive intelligence, client development and retention, and more. The accompanying CD-ROM contains a wealth of policies, statements, and other sample documents. If you're serious about improving the way your firm works, increasing productivity, making better decisions, and setting your firm on the right course, this book is the resource you need.

The Successful Lawyer: Powerful Strategies for Transforming Your Practice

By Gerald A. Riskin

Available as a Book, Audio-CD Set, or Combination Package.

Global management consultant and trusted advisor to many of the world's largest law firms, Gerry Riskin goes beyond simple concept or theory and delivers a book packed with practical advice that you can implement right away. By using the principles found in this book, you can live out your dreams, embrace success, and awaken your firm to its full potential. Large law firm or small, managing partners and associates in every area of practice—all can benefit from the information contained in this book. With this book, you can attract what you need and desire into your life, get more satisfaction from your practice and your clients, and do so in a systematic, achievable way.

How to Start and Build a Law Practice, Platinum Fifth Edition

By Jay G Foonberg

This classic ABA bestseller has been used by tens of thousands of lawyers as the comprehensive guide to planning, launching, and growing a successful practice. It's packed with over 600 pages of guidance on identifying the right location, finding clients, setting fees, managing your office, maintaining an ethical and responsible practice, maximizing available resources, upholding your standards, and much more. You'll find the information you need to successfully launch your practice, run it at maximum efficiency, and avoid potential pitfalls along the way. If you're committed to starting—and growing—your own practice, this one book will give you the expert advice you need to make it succeed for years to come.

Flying Solo: A Survival Guide for Solo and Small Firm Lawyers, Fourth Edition

Edited by K. William Gibson

This fourth edition of this comprehensive guide includes practical information gathered from a wide range of contributors, including successful solo practitioners, law firm consultants, state and local bar practice management advisors, and law school professors. This classic ABA book first walks you through a step-by-step analysis of the decision to start a solo practice, including choosing a practice focus. It then provides tools to help you with financial issues including banking and billing; operations issues such as staffing and office location and design decisions; technology for the small law office; and marketing and client relations. Whether you're thinking of going solo, new to the solo life, or a seasoned practitioner, *Flying Solo* provides time-tested answers to real-life questions.

30-Day Risk-Free Order Form
Call Today! 1-800-285-2221
Monday–Friday, 7:30 AM – 5:30 PM, Central Time

Qty	Title	LPM Price	Regular Price	Total
_____	The Lawyer's Guide to Collaboration Tools and Technologies: Smart Ways to Work Together (5110589)	$59.95	$ 89.95	$_____
_____	The Lawyer's Guide to Marketing on the Internet, Third Edition (5110585)	74.95	84.95	$_____
_____	The Lawyer's Field Guide to Effective Business Development (5110578)	49.95	59.95	$_____
_____	The Electronic Evidence and Discovery Handbook: Forms, Checklists, and Guidelines (5110569)	99.95	129.95	$_____
_____	The Lawyer's Guide to Extranets: Breaking Down Walls, Building Client Connections (5110494)	59.95	69.95	$_____
_____	The Law Firm Associate's Guide to Personal Marketing and Selling Skills (5110582)	39.95	49.95	$_____
_____	Trainer's Manual for the Law Firm Associate's Guide to Personal Marketing and Selling Skills (5110581)	49.95	59.95	$_____
_____	The Lawyer's Guide to Marketing Your Practice, Second Edition (5110500)	79.95	89.95	$_____
_____	The Lawyer's Guide to Increasing Revenue (5110521)	59.95	79.95	$_____
_____	The Lawyer's Guide to Strategic Planning (5110520)	59.95	79.95	$_____
_____	The Successful Lawyer: Powerful Strategies for Transforming Your Practice (5110531)	64.95	84.95	$_____
_____	How to Start and Build a Law Practice, Platinum Fifth Edition (5110508)	57.95	69.95	$_____
_____	Flying Solo: A Survival Guide for Solo and Small Firm Lawyers, Fourth Edition (5110527)	79.95	99.95	$_____

*Postage and Handling	
$10.00 to $24.99	$5.95
$25.00 to $49.99	$9.95
$50.00 to $99.99	$12.95
$100.00 to $349.99	$17.95
$350 to $499.99	$24.95

**Tax
DC residents add 5.75%
IL residents add 9.00%

*Postage and Handling $_____
**Tax $_____
TOTAL $_____

PAYMENT

❑ Check enclosed (to the ABA)

❑ Visa   ❑ MasterCard   ❑ American Express

_____
Account Number   Exp. Date   Signature

Name _____ Firm _____
Address _____
City _____ State _____ Zip _____
Phone Number _____ E-Mail Address _____

Guarantee

If—for any reason—you are not satisfied with your purchase, you may return it within 30 days of receipt for a complete refund of the price of the book(s). No questions asked!

Mail: ABA Publication Orders, P.O. Box 10892, Chicago, Illinois 60610-0892
♦ Phone: 1-800-285-2221 ♦ FAX: 312-988-5568

E-Mail: abasvcctr@abanet.org ♦ Internet: http://www.lawpractice.org/catalog

Are You in Your Element?

Tap into the Resources of the ABA Law Practice Management Section

ABA Law Practice Management Section Membership Benefits

The ABA Law Practice Management Section (LPM) is a professional membership organization of the American Bar Association that helps lawyers and other legal professionals with the business of practicing law. LPM focuses on providing information and resources in the core areas of marketing, management, technology, and finance through its award-winning magazine, teleconference series, Webzine, educational programs (CLE), Web site, and publishing division. For more than thirty years, LPM has established itself as a leader within the ABA and the profession-at-large by producing the world's largest legal technology conference (ABA TECHSHOW®) each year. In addition, LPM's publishing program is one of the largest in the ABA, with more than eighty-five titles in print.

In addition to significant book discounts, LPM Section membership offers these benefits:

ABA TECHSHOW
Membership includes a $100 discount to ABA TECHSHOW, the world's largest legal technology conference & expo!

Teleconference Series
Convenient, monthly CLE teleconferences on hot topics in marketing, management, technology and finance. Access educational opportunities from the comfort of your office chair – today's practical way to earn CLE credits!

Law Practice Magazine
Eight issues of our award-winning *Law Practice* magazine, full of insightful articles and practical tips on Marketing/Client Development, Practice Management, Legal Technology, and Finance.

Law Practice Today
LPM's unique Web-based magazine covers all the hot topics in law practice management today — identify current issues, face today's challenges, find solutions quickly. Visit www.lawpracticetoday.org.

Law Technology Today
LPM's newest Webzine focuses on legal technology issues in law practice management — covering a broad spectrum of the technology, tools, strategies and their implementation to help lawyers build a successful practice. Visit www.lawtechnologytoday.org.

LawPractice.news
LawPractice.news
Monthly news and information from the ABA Law Practice Management Section

LawPractice.news
Brings Section news, educational opportunities, book releases, and special offers to members via e-mail each month.

To learn more about the ABA Law Practice Management Section, visit www.lawpractice.org or call 1-800-285-2221.